Becoming Conscious

Helen Adams

Note for Librarians: A cataloguing record for this book is available from Library and Archives Canada at www.collectionscanada.ca/amicus/index-e.html

ISBN 1-4120-9459-3

Printed in Victoria, BC, Canada. Printed on paper with minimum 30% recycled fibre. Trafford's print shop runs on "green energy" from solar, wind and other environmentally-friendly power sources.

Offices in Canada, USA, Ireland and UK

Book sales for North America and international:
Trafford Publishing, 6E–2333 Government St.,
Victoria, BC V8T 4P4 CANADA
phone 250 383 6864 (toll-free 1 888 232 4444)
fax 250 383 6804; email to orders@trafford.com

Book sales in Europe:
Trafford Publishing (UK) Limited, 9 Park End Street, 2nd Floor
Oxford, UK OX1 1HH UNITED KINGDOM
phone +44 (0)1865 722 113 (local rate 0845 230 9601)
facsimile +44 (0)1865 722 868; info.uk@trafford.com

Order online at:
trafford.com/06-1214

10 9 8 7 6 5

TABLE OF CONTENTS

INTRODUCTION

What is life all about?

I began writing this book because I see most people living their lives in an ignorance of what their lives are about and what their life path is. I wanted to change that somehow and show people how they can become more conscious of their lives.

After doing hundreds of horoscopes for people, I have reached the inevitable conclusion that the planets in the Solar System do have an effect on life on Earth, and your life. That is whether you know it or not, or even whether you like it or not.

In my experience of it Astrology does work – if it didn't some of the finest minds on the Planet, as well as myself wouldn't persist with it!

It saddens me that Astrology is discredited, invalidated and trivialised in newspapers and magazines by its use in a commercial sense, making it meaningless and worthless.

This book has been written so every individual can take back their personal power and spiritual heritage. The information and techniques within these pages can be used to reconnect you to the natural (yo)universe that you are one with.

Astrology is a system of analysis that can be utilised to supply an individual with VITAL LIFE INFORMATION so their life can be lived in greater conscious awareness of:-

THE LIFE PURPOSE

THE LIFE LESSONS

THE LIFE TALENTS AND GIFTS

THE LIFE FEARS, INHIBITIONS AND KARMA

THE ORIGINS OF CERTAIN BEHAVIOURS

Just imagine if we had this kind of information from the start of our lives, how different our lives would have been. I am sure that there is absolutely no one that can't be helped and assisted to live a more fulfilling life by this book.

"Ignorance isn't bliss, it's oblivion." Philip Wylie.
Generation of Vipers.

PART I

CHAPTER ONE

THE 12 SIGNS WHICH MAKE UP THE 6 POLARITIES

It gives me immense pleasure to present to you the 12 signs in an in-depth study.

When you read through them you will see just how they inter-connect to so many other things that you may not have previously associated them with.

These are the take home notes I distribute to my students. So, as they go through each sign, learning about these archetypes of human behaviour, they relate it to themselves to see if they are using the energies of the sign well, or badly.

This is very empowering self-knowledge indeed.

You see the horoscope is a circle and has 12 houses with each sign on or in one of these houses.

SO WE ARE EACH MADE UP OF ALL THE 12 SIGNS TO GREATER OR

LESSER DEGREES – NOT JUST YOUR SUN SIGN.

I hope you enjoy learning about your Sun Sign, which is the identity you are learning to become, your special area of personal potential, and how you can SHINE in this world and in your life. The Sun Sign is the style, if you like of how you can become self-realised, and the house position is the field of experience it can occurr in.

Also, since no one lives in isolation and we all contact many people in our lives, whether that is because of biological or circumstantial reasons, knowing about ALL the signs gives us a good education about life generally.

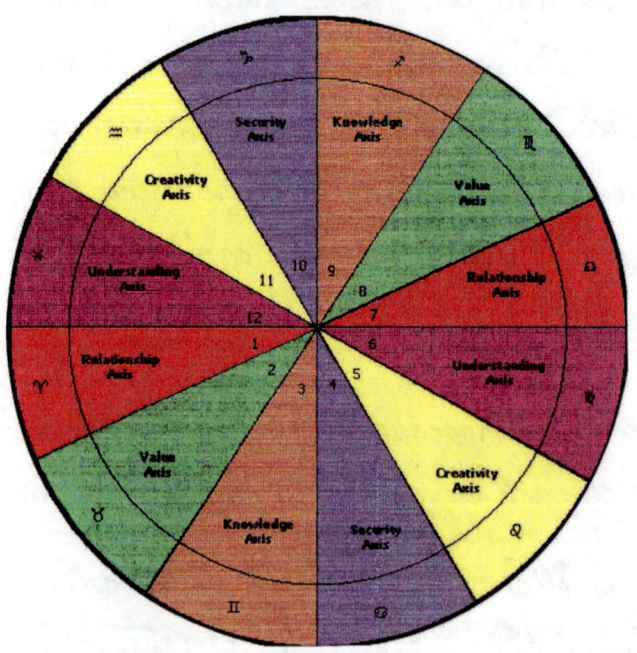

THE 12 SIGNS OF THE ZODIAC WHICH MAKE UP THE 6 POLARITIES

ARIES

I SEEK MYSELF

Aries is closely associated and ruled by the fiery red planet Mars. Aries rules the first house of the zodiac and is the opposite sign to Libra, which rules the opposite house, the Seventh house. Aries and the First House is the bottom half of the RELATIONSHIP AXIS.

Keywords for Aries are:-

Positive +: action initiating, pioneering, energetic, decisive, outgoing.

Negative -: aggressive, fool hardy, pushy, hot headed, macho, impatient.

The symbol for Aries is the ram and Aries is masculine or positive (external), a fire sign and cardinal in nature. Aries is the search for the separate identity, the I AM principle.

The physical rulership to parts of the body are — the head, the face (except the nose), and the brain.

The general traits of the sign of Aries are on the positive side —inspirational and courageous and on the negative side to be impulsive and rebellious.

THE CENTRAL ISSUE THAT ARIES NEEDS TO LEARN IS PATIENCE.

Spiritual development is brought about with and through SELF-AWARENESS and SELF-DEVELOPMENT.

Aries is also symbolic of new growth and independence

In the house of the zodiac where Aries rules the cusp is where you need to grow and develop. There is a need to learn and discover for yourself. New things will be started all the time.

If you do not have your own personal horoscope this can be easily obtained from many sites on the internet for free. Because society is becoming more free-thinking, there is much more Astrological information and classes available for those who are interested in learning about the life-process and your own particular experience of life, through the study of *ASTROLOGY*.

The evolution of the sign of Aries from undeveloped to developed is a journey from the negative qualities to the positive in the course of as many lives as it takes.

WHO AM I?

Aries is very self-concerned because the Aries person is very unaware of themselves (emotionally, as their orientation is more physical)and the impact that they have on others and their own life.

In the undeveloped stages it is not surprising that the qualities of being brazen, forceful, bumptious and overly independent and unco-operative often present problems in relating to others.

When there is unmitigated expression of physical urges and energy there is difficulty in pacing themselves so they fluctuate between over enthusiasm to burnout. The Aries impatience often leads them to not complete what they have started, dropping it and starting something else.

So its going from free wheeling adventures and the

novelty of the new or risk-taking, to making a positive contribution by using the qualities of an unshakable belief in themselves and the courage and strength within to motivate themselves and others towards the challenges that life has to offer, supporting others to heights of achievement through their own example.

ASTROLOGY AND CRYSTALS.

The Aries energy can be greatly assisted in its development by the use of the following crystals:

Bloodstone: This is for grounding the fire and for grounded self-confidence.

Garnet: This is for the awareness of self as viable and competent.

Tiger Eye: This aids in clear seeing and courage and stimulates personal power and integrity.

THE FLOWER REMEDIES AND ASTROLOGY

The following are Australian Bush Flower Essences that specifically assist the development of the Aries qualities to be expressed positively. They are however merely suggestions:-

Mountain Devil — This essence deals with anger/ aggression and converts these things to happiness and love.

Black-eyed Susan — This tones down temper/frustration and bustling activity for more inner peace.

Kangaroo Paw — This is for relating to others and the awareness of the impact on others.

ESSENTIAL OILS

Black Pepper, Clove, Coriander, Ginger, Cumin, Petitgrain and Pine.

ASTROLOGY AND THE TAROT

The association of the zodiac signs with the Tarot cards has always been, although not widely known! It is my hope that this connection can be used by anyone with the intention that self knowledge is self empowering, and as a tool for self growth. The deck used is the Thoth deck.

The Tarot cards associated with the sign of Aries are: -

The Emperor, The Tower, The Ace of Wands, The Queen of Wands, The Princess of Disks, 2 of Wands,

3 of Disks, 3 of Wands, 4 of Wands, 5 of Cups, 7 of Wands, 9 of Swords, and 10 of Cups.

The 3 of Wands is the Sun in Aries and it is called "Virtue". Although the colour red is prominent in this card the colour orange is even more prominent. After some contemplation of this I realised that orange was the colour of relationships and this was there because the opposite polarity of the card (Libra) is the sign of relating. To hold ones centre is the greatest contribution one can make to a relationship. Aries, although independent/alone, must still operate with and through and for others. So the other side of the sign of the ONE is the co-operation and presence of the other. Independence within a relationship.

I found the yellow colour of the 3 of Wands to be symbolic of inspiration towards mental energies — thought. Inspiring the individual to have self awareness of their part in the human drama.

The 3 of Wands has the red flames radiating out from the centre inspiring the spirit to individual action springing out from the all-that-is. The flames licking out seem to intuit life and vitality — a positivity towards a virtuous act of courage and bravado. The flowers at the end of the wands seem to imply a blossoming of one's potentials or a self-development through just being your true self.

THE SPIRITUAL LESSON OF ARIES

The Aries spiritual lesson is about LOVE. LOVE IN ACTION. Learning to think before acting. Understanding the needs and feelings of others.

ASTROLOGY AND NUMEROLOGY

The astrology signs all have association and affinities with the numbers in Numerology. Even though there are 12 signs and only 9 numbers don't forget the master numbers are included and very important

The number associated with Aries and also the planet Mars is the NUMBER ONE.

The keyword for the number One is ACTIVATION.

Number ONE has the qualities of leadership - the one who leads the way. The power is in the ability to take the initiative. However assertion and not aggression is the way to go. These people are the self-starters, the ones who take things on.

Positive Keywords are — individuality, courage, energy, self-determination.

Negative Keywords are — knowing it all, egotism, bossy, wilfulness, contrariness.

Some of the things that Aries rules are: - adrenalin, hats, fire, sharp instruments and surgical operations.

Aries people enjoy any work requiring enterprise and initiative, such as — medicine, surgeons, dentists, athletes, steel workers, military, politics, anything that is of a pioneering nature as they like to be 'first' or lead the way in new things.

Countries ruled by Aries are: - England, Germany, Denmark, Palestine and Burgundy.

Cities ruled by Aries are: - Florence, Naples, Verona, Marseilles, Birmingham, Ancient Athens and Sparta.

Peoples ruled by Aries are: - Jews and Muslims.

Plants ruled by Aries are: - Radish, rhubarb,

peppers, garlic, hemp, broom, holly, thistle, nettles, onions and mustard.

TAURUS

I SEEK MYSELF THROUGH WHAT I HAVE

Taurus is closely associated and ruled by the planet Venus, it is feminine and negative, (receptive or internal). Taurus rules the Second House of the zodiac and is opposite to the sign of Scorpio, which rules the opposite house, the Eighth House. Taurus and the Second House are the bottom half of the VALUE AXIS.

Keywords for Taurus are:-

Positive +: persevering, reliable, acquisitive, practical, trustworthy.

Negative -: possessive, jealous, lazy, stubborn, extravagant.

The symbol for Taurus is the bull and Taurus is an earth sign, which is fixed. Taurus rules the Second House of the zodiac.

Taurus is the search for value, inner security and self-worth.

The physical rulership to parts of the body are — the

neck, throat and the ears. Taurus has an affinity with the lymphatic system of the body and the thyroid gland also comes under the Taurean rulership.

The general traits of the sign of Taurus are on the positive side- steadfast and loyal, productive and fertile, and on the negative side — stingy, rigid and seeks only material rewards for efforts.

THE CENTRAL ISSUE THAT TAURUS NEEDS TO LEARN IS DETACHMENT.

Spiritual development is brought about through the use of detachment to understand that security comes from within, not through possessions or material things.

In the house of the zodiac where Taurus rules the cusp is where you need to be productive and see the actual results of your productivity.

The evolution of the sign of Taurus from undeveloped to developed is a journey from the negative qualities to the positive in the course of as many lives as it takes.

WHAT IS MY WORTH?

Taureans are very resistant to change and since change is the only constant in life, they wear themselves out being stubborn and rigid. The undeveloped Taurean usually digs a rut for themself, which they hope deepens, offering the "security" they want. Taurus is ruled by Venus so with the connection of this planet to art and beauty this often tempts them out of the rut to express these talents, and also appreciate the talents of others making them connoisseurs of life, who make an art of the sensual pleasures. Taurus is an earth sign, which is of the physical so attending to the physical comforts and providing for their physical needs comes more easily to them. Developed Taureans have the ability to create things of value and to share their productivity with others, who are less adept at creating it, becoming the cheerful giver.

ASTROLOGY AND CRYSTALS

The Taurus energy can be greatly assisted in its development by the use of the following crystals:

Petrified Wood: This captures the Taurean essence and aids the connection with nature.

Carnelian: This stone helps give a positive self-image and self esteem.

Jade: This is for prosperity, fertility and longevity.

THE FLOWER REMEDIES AND ASTROLOGY

The following are Australian Bush Flower Essences that specifically assist the development of the Taurus qualities to be expressed positively.

Bauhinia — For resistance to change, and those people in a rut that have a rigidity and reluctance to move ahead.

Dog Rose — For insecurity and to give more self-confidence and a belief in self.

Five Corners — For more self-worth and a better self value system with a celebration of their own beauty

ESSENTIAL OILS

Cardamom, Lilac, Rose, Vetivert, Ylang Ylang and Gardenia.

ASTROLOGY AND THE TAROT

The Tarot cards associated with the sign of Taurus and the planet Venus are: -

The Empress, The Hierophant, The Ace of Disks, The Prince of Disks, 2 of Cups, 5 of Swords, 5 of Disks, 6 of Disks, 7 of Disks, 7 of Cups, and 9 of Disks.

The Hierophant No. 5 of the Major Arcana.

The symbol of the bull seems to evoke a feeling of strength that comes from the inner depths. The strength to be solid, dependable and reliable. The weight of the bull would indicate a slowness, a plodding which could cause a state of perpetual stagnation (fixidity). The five pointed star which is superimposed seems to say that it's the human being (head, legs, arms —5). So a feeling of being very physical and grounded or earthy is projected. Also, from the very heavy colours on the card there is a dense 'down-to-earth' practicality — a simple outlook/enduring.

The priestess may indicate a feminine aspect or to let your inner urgings through — the feminine (in both females AND MALES) voice is so soft/magnetic that you have to LISTEN for it.

Taurus in Astrology rules the neck/throat so the voice, both speaking and singing, is a vehicle for enlightenment or upliftment. The enquirer that draws this card is seeking spiritual guidance and a meeting with such a person is possible. The *Hierophant* who brings the light of consciousness into the darkness of ignorance.

THE SPIRITUAL LESSON OF TAURUS

The *Taurus* spiritual lesson is one of learning about SERVICE. Service through building — lessons are learned through owning or losing property. Learning to realise that possessions are to be enjoyed but not worshipped. Learning to be a cheerful giver.

ASTROLOGY AND NUMEROLOGY

The number associated with *Taurus* and also the planet Venus is the NUMBER FOUR.

The keyword for the number Four is SECURITY.

Number FOUR people are the practical workers and their power is in their endurance. Fours are reliable and have the ability to create order out of chaos. They are the 'salt-of-the-earth' types. This number concentrates on work/order/foundations/ and the body.

Positive Keywords are — productivity, strength, gratitude, worthiness, and endurance.

Negative Keywords are — jealousy, dullness, crudeness, plodding, and narrowness.

Some of the things that Taurus rules are: - architecture, banks, jewellery, music, purses and wallets.

Taurus people enjoy any routine work such as accountants, farmers, consultants, artists, real estate, building and finance.

Countries ruled by Taurus are: - Ireland, Russia, Switzerland (known for the centre of international banking), Poland, Cyprus, Persia and Crete.

Plants ruled by Taurus are: - Moss, spinach, lilies, daisies, dandelions, beets, larkspur and myrtle.

GEMINI

I SEEK MYSELF THROUGH WHAT I THINK

Gemini is closely associated and ruled by the planet Mercury, it is masculine (external) and an air sign. Gemini rules the Third House of the zodiac and is the opposite sign to Sagittarius, which rules the opposite house, the Ninth House. Gemini and the Third House are the bottom half of the KNOWLEDGE AXIS.

Keywords for Gemini are:-

Positive +: versatile, intellectual, friendly, witty, studious, dextrous.

Negative -: restless, two-faced, contradictory, superficial, gossiping.

The symbol for Gemini is the twins. Gemini is an air sign and of mutable expression. Gemini rules the Third House of the zodiac.

Gemini is the search for information and how to communicate.

Physical rulership to parts of the body are- shoulders,

arms, hands, lungs, thymus gland and oxygenation of the body through breathing.

The general traits of the sign of Gemini are on the positive side- inquisitive and versatile and on the negative side- inconsistent and scattered.

THE CENTRAL ISSUE THAT GEMINI NEEDS TO LEARN IS MENTAL FOCUS.

Spiritual development is brought about with and through education, learning and communicating. Learning to listen and move easily in their communities.

In the house of the horoscope where Gemini rules the cusp is where you need to be curious or inquisitive. Your curiosity will help you grow through your experiences.

The evolution of the sign of Gemini from undeveloped to developed is a journey from the negative qualities to the positive in the course of as many lives as it takes.

HOW DO I THINK?

The undeveloped Gemini gets caught in a web of meaningless trivia and has a very short attention span. This web of trivia and time wasting non-sense can overwork the nervous system to breakdown if this style of living is not overcome. Just becoming conscious that this lifestyle is counter productive gives them the ability to leave it behind and move towards focusing their mental abilities and slowing the thought processes down. Gemini rules the lungs, so breathing techniques can be used to bring their consciousness into the present and not scattered everywhere. Slowing down the thoughts will give clarity and more time to think.

The developed Gemini energy makes wonderful teachers as they have learned how to communicate (by listening) to others the knowledge they have acquired and pass it on to others who are curious to learn.

ASTROLOGY AND CRYSTALS

The Gemini energy can be greatly assisted in its development by the use of the following crystals.

Agate: This is for mental energy, study and communication.

Amazonite: This is to harmonise the mental processes and creative flow.

Citrine: This stone is for mental clarity.

THE FLOWER REMEDIES AND

ASTROLOGY

The following are Australian Bush Flower Essences that specifically assist the development of the Gemini qualities to be expressed positively. They are however merely suggestions: -

Boronia - To relieve mental exhaustion and over-thinking.

Jacaranda — For mental scatteredness and give instead clarity of thought and mental focus.

Bush Fuchsia — For learning difficulties.

ESSENTIAL OILS

Lavender, Lemon Grass, Peppermint, Rosemary, Clary Sage.

ASTROLOGY AND THE TAROT

The Tarot cards associated with the sign of Gemini are: -

The Magician, The Lovers, The Ace of Swords, The Knight of Swords, 3 of Cups, 5 of Disks, 6 of Swords, 8 of Swords, 8 of Wands, 10 of Swords, and 10 of Disks.

The Lovers card No. 6 of the Major Arcana. The duality of this card is so strongly indicated as there is two of everything. The veiled figure presiding over the man and woman lovers seems to indicate that all is not as it seems, or they are 'controlled' by a exterior force of some kind or there is a 'trick' to it.

I feel the highest expression of this card is the inner marriage of masculine and feminine (regardless of gender).

"To be or not to be" that is the quest! Decision Vs Indecision. Truth Vs lie. Fun Vs meaning, etc., etc. The lion and the eagle seem to be saying Glory Vs power. Superficiality Vs depth. The egg and the snake would seem to say transformation/change through marriage/partnership.

There's a lack of permanency, a temporary situation that is changeable at any moment without warning causing a feeling of confusion, mental scattiness and indecision — nothing matters too much because it wont last anyway. The Mercurial influence of quicksilver is very strong. You must get what you can from each moment.

THE SPIRITUAL LESSON OF GEMINI

The Gemini spiritual lesson is one of learning about BROTHERHOOD. BROTHERHOOD through the spirit. Gemini people need to learn to develop their powers of concentration and steadfastness, training and controlling the everyday mind, so that it becomes illuminated and strengthened by the HIGHER consciousness.

ASTROLOGY AND NUMEROLOGY

The number associated with Gemini and also the planet Mercury is the NUMBER THREE.

The keyword for the number Three is EXPANSION.

Number THREE has the magical power or the ability to spread joy to those around it. Their creativity is high and they are very positive and popular socially because of their eloquence of speech and powers of expression. Because of their expansive nature, they meet people from different cultures and social strata, increasing their already broad thinking. These people must take care not to scatter their energies too much or spread themselves too thin.

Positive keywords are — optimism, kindness, artistic, imagination, inspirational.

Negative keywords are - worrying, gossiping, triviality, exaggeration, vanity.

Some of the things Gemini rules are: - automobiles, books, computers, messages and post offices.

Gemini people enjoy any work with variety. They like anything to do with a number of different environments or travel. Some careers associated with this sign are: - sales, journalists, transportation, communications, teaching, advertising or languages.

Countries ruled by Gemini are: - United States, Belgium, Wales, Sardinia, North East Coast of Africa, Lower Egypt.

Cities are: - London, Melbourne, San Francisco, Cardoba, Versailles, Plymouth, Nuremberg and Cardiff.

Plants ruled by Gemini are: - Yarrow, woodbine, vervain, tansy.

CANCER

I SEEK MYSELF THROUGH WHAT I FEEL

Cancer is closely associated with and ruled by the Moon. Cancer rules the Fourth House of the zodiac and is the opposite sign to Capricorn, which rules the Tenth house. Cancer and the Fourth House are the bottom half of the SECURITY AXIS.

Keywords for Cancer are:-

Positive +; nurturing, feeling, caring, protective, reflective/receptive.

Negative -; insecure, clinging, immature, oversensitive, attached.

The symbol for Cancer is the crab and Cancer is a feminine (internal) water sign and cardinal in expression.

Cancer is the search for the self through the emotions or the feeling nature.

Physical rulership is:- stomach, breast, digestion and the uterus.

The general traits of the sign of Cancer are on the positive side — Holds the family together, cares for others needs and wants and on the negative side — is non-progressive and has unfounded fears.

THE CENTRAL ISSUE THAT CANCER NEEDS TO LEARN IS TO LET GO.

Spiritual development is brought about by learning that emotional security comes from within.

Cancer is symbolic of the 'Peak of Achievement'. In the house of the zodiac where Cancer rules the cusp is where you need growth through instruction and training. This house tells you where you need to use the positive qualities of your Sun sign.

The evolution of the sign of Cancer is one of the most difficult because of its rulership by the Moon and its emotional influences from past lives. The evolutionary progress from undeveloped to developed is a journey from the negative qualities to the positive in the course of as many lives as it takes.

WHERE DO I BELONG?

Cancer is about learning how to care for and nurture,

and the best way to learn this is to be cared for lovingly by others. Consequently, the early Cancer lifetimes are ones of dependency. The undeveloped Cancer qualities are ones of emotional manipulation of others to avoid situations that they fear, or to use family restrictions as an excuse not to achieve in the outside world. Eventually they move beyond emotional dependency to emotional security from within, which is based on a mutual caring and sharing from each family member to create the circumstances to achieve emotional stability. In this state they are ideally suited to nurturing others in the professions of nursing or the hospitality industry, not to mention their many psychic and intuitive talents and gifts.

ASTROLOGY AND CRYSTALS FOR THE SIGN OF CANCER

The Cancer energy can be greatly assisted in its development by the use of the following crystals:

Blue Lace Agate:- This stone clarifies emotional needs and calms.

Moonstone:- This stone is for nurturing/domestic issues/birthing.

Smokey Quartz:- This stone is for mother issues and dissipates subtle energy blocks caused by negative emotions or fears.

THE FLOWER REMEDIES AND ASTROLOGY

The following are Australian Bush Flower Essences that specifically assist the development of the Cancer qualities to be expressed positively. They are however merely suggestions:-

Bottlebrush — For the ability to let go and also for nurturing skills

Dog Rose of the Wild Forces — For emotional balance and support to allow release of held-in emotions.

Boab — To disconnect from family patterns and ascend.

Red Suva Frangipani — For emotional turmoil from grief or loss, and also relationship emotional upheavals.

ESSENTIAL OILS

Camphor, Jasmine, Rose and Sandalwood.

ASTROLOGY AND THE TAROT.

The Tarot cards associated with the sign of Cancer and the Moon are:-

The Chariot, The Moon, The Priestess, The Queen of Cups, The Knight of Cups, The Ace of Cups, 2 of Swords, 4 of Cups, 6 of Disks, 7 of Swords.

The Chariot No. 7 of the Major Arcana. With this card the very first thing that was apparent was the over pre-occupation with "protection". Feeling safe seems to be an issue. The armoured man is holding a disk of energy at the position of the stomach —Cancer rules the stomach in the physical body. The colour of blue, which is the colour of the emotions, is pushed to the outside of the card — would this indicate that they are too much to cope with? The colour red however is at the core of the disk indicating inner frustrations and anger held in. Cancerians are very susceptible to stomach ulcers from held in angers etc. The card also seems to signify an urgency to be ambitious or successful, a desire for triumph. With all that protective armour and defences it would be difficult to get through to those of the sign of Cancer or for them to overcome their emotional fears.

THE SPRIRITUAL LESSON OF CANCER

The Cancerian Spiritual Lesson is about PEACE. PEACE IN ACTION. Learning to Let Go of outcomes and have the emotional security to handle lifes ups and downs. Trusting that your life will provide you with the nurturance you require.

ASTROLOGY AND NUMEROLOGY

The number associated with Cancer and also the Moon is the NUMBER TWO.

The keyword for the number Two is ATTRACTION.

Number TWO people are the peacemakers, counsellors, and supporters. Two is a feminine energy which is intuitive and sensitive and they are naturally tuned into the moods and feeling of others. Their power is in their diplomacy. However they need to be aware of the possibility of becoming a fence sitter and a doormat. and need to avoid feelings of inferiority.

Positive Keywords are – gentleness, harmony, receptivity, charm, rhythm, and consideration for others.

Negative Keywords are — pessimism, sulkiness, apathy, slyness and deception.

Some of the things that Cancer rules are ;- bakeries, boats, buildings, lakes and plumbing.

Cancer people enjoy any work connected with the sea, liquids, catering for public tastes, or supplying domestic needs. Some of the careers are — social workers, antique dealers, comedians, shop keepers, food industry, laundry, hotels and the accommodation industry.

Countries ruled by Cancer are;- Scotland, Holland, Paraguay, New Zealand and Most of Africa.

Cities are;- New York, Constantinople, Venice, Genoa, Stockholm, Tunis, Algiers, Amsterdam, Manchester and Milan.

Peoples are:- Indigenous Africans.

Plants ruled by Cancer are;- cucumbers, squashes, melons, all plants that grow in the water, waterlilies and rushes.

LEO

I SEEK MYSELF THROUGH WHAT I CREATE

Leo is closely associated and ruled by the Sun. Leo rules the Fifth House of the zodiac and is the opposite sign to Aquarius, which rules the Eleventh House. Leo and the Fifth House are the bottom half of the CREATIVITY AXIS.

Keywords for Leo are: –

Positive +: Loving, centering, creative, childlike, generous

Negative –: Demanding, overbearing, self-glorifying, egotistical, attention seeking.

The symbol for Leo is the Lion and Leo is a masculine, positive (external) sign and fixed in nature.

Leo is the search for creative self-expression.

The physical rulership to parts of the body are — the heart, back, spine, vitality, body heat and perspiration.

The general traits of the sign of Leo are on the positive side — warm and sincere, artistic and expressive and on the negative side — lustful, hedonistic and falsely modest.

THE CENTRAL ISSUE THAT LEO NEEDS TO LEARN IS HUMILITY

Spiritual development is brought about by learning to let their spirit shine through their heart centre — self-expression!

In the house of the zodiac where Leo rules the cusp is where you feel a need for "personal development". If you are using the positive qualities of your Sun Sign in the affairs of this house, you will feel a deep sense of inner peace and contentment.

The evolution of the sign of Leo from undeveloped to developed is a journey from the negative qualities to the positive in the course of as many lives as it takes.

HOW DO I LOVE?

The undeveloped Leos are self-centred and narcissistic — enthralled and pre-occupied with themselves and their abilities. If it were otherwise though, they might not bother with self-development and self-expression. All this self-absorption and the desire for attention and power urges them to seek the spotlight.

The negative qualities of the sign of Leo are the negative ego expressing itself. In the course of the early undeveloped lifetimes the negative qualities persist only because the ego is weak and needs re-assurance. Once the ego begins to strengthen and gain confidence and self-assurance the defences drop enough for the heart centre to open and radiate love, also allowing creativity to flow through it.

Leo has the capacity to shine and lead others in any creative endeavour, particularly with children and those needing encouragement. They make excellent leaders, teachers and coaches, and have capabilities that inspire others who bask in their warmth and generosity.

ASTROLOGY AND CRYSTALS

The Leo energy can be greatly assisted in its development by the use of the following crystals:

Amber: This stone is fossilized sunshine — for vitality.

Kunzite: This stone is for self-acceptance.

Rose Quartz: This stone is for love and creativity, and to open the heart chakra.

THE FLOWER REMEDIES AND ASTROLOGY

The following are Australian Bush Flower Essences that specifically assist the development of the Leo qualities to be expressed positively. They are however merely suggestions:-

Bluebell – For opening the heart to a belief in abundance and a universal trust and joyful sharing.

Gymea Lily – For humility that allows others to express themselves and contribute.

Little Flannel Flower – For joy and playfulness and spontaneity.

Turkey Bush – For removing creative blocks.

THE ESSENTIAL OILS

Basil, Cinnamon, Frankincense, Lime, Neroli, Orange and Nasturtium.

ASTROLOGY AND THE TAROT

The Tarot cards associated with the sign of Leo are:-

The Sun, No. 11 Lust, The Prince of Wands, 5 of

Wands, 7 of Wands, 3 of Wands, 4 of Disks, 6 of Cups and 8 of Disks.

The *LUST* card, which has the colour of gold, royal expensive, regal gold — fit for kings and queens! The very large lion seems to imply masculine strength — bravado and largesse. The naked woman suggests an openness — an attitude of courage to be one self with pride and nothing to hide. The ruling planet is the Sun and the woman is holding a fire (the Sun) in one hand only, so she is powerful and assured of herself — confidence abounds. The physical vitality and energy to lead others to creative heights. 'Lust' indulges in the pleasures of re-creation and creativity of one in touch with the spirit of life. The card of strength.

THE SPIRITUAL LESSON OF LEO

The Leo spiritual lesson is about *LOVE. LOVE THROUGH CREATIVITY* — using the mind in the heart. Learning through sorrow in affections. Learning through matters connected to the Fifth House of the zodiac, creativity, children, recreating, expression, pleasure, ego.

ASTROLOGY AND NUMEROLOGY

The number associated with Leo and also the Sun is the *NUMBER FIVE.*

The keyword for the number Five is *EXPERIENCE.*

The number *FIVE* needs freedom so that it can indulge its senses in the experience of life. The power of the Five lies in knowing how to deal constructively with the desire for freedom.

Positive Keywords are — lively, entertaining, promotive, progressive, adaptable.

Negative Keywords are — restless, flashy, discontented, hedonistic, indulgent.

Some of the things that Leo rules are :- cards, entertainment, forests, ovens and stadiums.

Leo people enjoy work that gives them scope for their creativity, their organisational ability, or for self-exploitation. Some of the careers are — jewellers, acting, teaching, sport (professional), sales, or the military.

Countries ruled by Leo are:- France, Italy, Sicily, Romania, Bohemia.

Cities ruled by Leo are:- Rome, Prague, Damascus, Bombay, Bath, Chicago, Philadelphia and Los Angeles.

Plants ruled by Leo are:- daffodil, marigold, sunflowers, poppy, fennel and parsley.

VIRGO

I SEEK MYSELF THROUGH WORK AND SERVICE

Virgo is closely associated and ruled by the planet Mercury. Virgo rules the Sixth House of the zodiac and is the opposite sign to Pisces, which rules the opposite house, the Twelfth House. Virgo is also ruled by the planetoid CHIRON that was discovered in 1977. Virgo and the Sixth House are the bottom half of the AXIS OF UNDERSTANDING.

Keywords for Virgo are: -

Positive+: analysing, useful, efficient, systematic, detailed.

Negative -: worrying, fault finding, fussy, nit-picking, skeptical.

The symbol for Virgo is the Virgin and Virgo is a feminine (internal) earth sign and mutable in expression.

The Physical rulership to parts of the body are- intestines, bowels, duodenum, food assimilation and hands.

The general traits of the sign of Virgo are on the

positive side — helpful and unassuming, precise and meticulous and the researcher and scientist. On the negative side — nervous and dependent, fault finding and intolerant.

THE CENTRAL ISSUE THAT VIRGO NEEDS TO LEARN IS TOLERENCE AND TO ACCEPT.

Spiritual development is through learning not to judge others and to develop healing attitudes instead of criticism.

In the house of the horoscope where Virgo rules the cusp is where you need to "discard the chaff from the wheat". There is a need to analyse your feelings with regard to the affairs of the house in a practical unemotional manner.

The evolution of the sign of Virgo from undeveloped to developed is a journey from the negative qualities to the positive in the course of as many lives as it takes.

HOW CAN I HEAL?

Early lifetimes as a Virgo are spent in servitude where efficiency and hard work are imposed on them and they do it out of necessity to survive. They fuss and worry that they won't be good enough. They may lose themselves not realising that they have the power to heal their own lives, and hard work is a celebration of that, as it is themselves who reap the benefits of their labours. To serve unconditionally with love and reverence and that helping others is in fact helping ourselves for the highest good of all, as we are all connected and part of the same continuum. So its learning the virtue of service and not to be enslaved by others that will ultimately heal the Virgo life. Responding to the faith (not fear) that when we heal ourselves we heal the planet and everything on it.

ASTROLOGY AND CRYSTALS

The Virgo energy can be greatly assisted in its positive development by the following crystals. They are however merely suggestions.

Agate — This stone is for mental energy and self-esteem.

Sodalite — This stone aids mental balance.

Lepidolite — This stone mitigates toxic fear and clarifies mental energy for inner work.

THE FLOWER REMEDIES AND ASTROLOGY

The following are Australian Bush Flower Essences that assist the positive development of Virgo qualities.

Yellow Cowslip Orchid - For nit-picking and being critical and judgmental

Philotheca- For those focused on giving and not receiving

Crowea — For worrying or stress, brings calm and balance

ESSENTIAL OILS

Clary Sage, Cypress, Fennel, Lemon Balm, and Dill.

ASTROLOGY AND THE TAROT.

The tarot cards associated with the sign of Virgo are:-

The Hermit, The Knight of Disks, The Queen of Swords, The 8 of Disks and the 10 of Disks.

The Virgo Card the 8 of Disks — Intelligence applied to material affairs! Mercury ruled Virgo is represented strongly with the yellow background (mental) with the tree growing in the earth (earth sign) saying that to be grounded and practical is essential. The name of the card "*Prudence*" is characteristic of Virgo as the sign of discrimination — to discriminate, analyse, sort/ organise into a system and method of productivity.

Physically the thick, strong tree trunk indicates healthiness and strong roots — a stability. So the major focus of the card is physical health and therefore the ability to work hard and long using mental energies to achieve success, which are indicated by the blossoming flowers. The element earth is present too as the sun is 'shining' down on the tree and the green grass giving "energy" to the materialistic goal(s) of the querant. The number 8 may mean its cyclic/perpetual/eternal, the sun beats down on the earth, making the plants grow to bear fruit/produce and the fruit drops off and a seed grows — on and on.........

THE SPIRITUAL LESSON OF VIRGO

The Virgo spiritual lesson is about SERVICE. Service by the power of the mind — every Virgo has a mission of service, either to the family or the world family. Learning the importance of the physical body as an instrument of the spirit, to serve at fullest capacity. (Always remember your family is a microcosm of the macrocosm. The universe is holographic).

ASTROLOGY AND NUMEROLOGY

The number associated with Virgo and Mercury and the planetoid Chiron is the number TWENTY TWO.

The keywords are: THE MASTER BUILDER.

The master number 22/4 are the practical idealists and therin lies their power. Balance is all important, along with equality of peoples and nations. In their highest expression they have learned mastery of spiritual values to create and build material abundance. If the lower 4 is reverted to, they must use personal power or the lack of as a guide until able to progress to the spiritual 22 energy.

Positive Keywords are: - practical idealism, internationally directed, on a mission of service to mankind.

Negative Keywords are: - Big talkers, dictatorial, into get-rich-quick schemes, dishonest.

Some of the things that Virgo rules are: - chemistry, craftsmanship, first aid, herbs and libraries.

Virgo people are happy in careers that demand technical

or analytical skill or that affords the opportunity of service. Some of the careers are medicine, health workers, chemists, administrators, accountants, teachers and systems analysts.

Countries ruled by Virgo are:- Crete, part of Greece, Croatia, Brazil, Turkey and the West Indies.

Cities are:- Jerusalem, Paris, Athens, Heidelberg, Boston, Strasbourg.

Plants that are ruled by Virgo are:- Endive, millet, corn, wheat, barley, oats, rye, valerian, skullcap.

LIBRA

I SEEK MYSELF THROUGH WHAT I UNITE.

Libra is closely associated and ruled by the planet Venus. Libra rules the Seventh House of the zodiac and is the opposite to Aries, which rules the opposite house, the First House. Libra is the top half of the RELATIONSHIP AXIS.

Keywords for Libra are:-

Positive +: balancing, harmonising, artistic, refined, social.

Negative-: indecisive, procrastinating, inconsistent, dependent on approval, lazy.

The symbol for Libra is the scales and Libra is an air sign and cardinal in expression. Libra is the search for harmony and balance.

The physical rulership to parts of the body are — the kidneys, ovaries and urine (filtration of body fluids).

The general traits of the sign of Libra are on the positive side — sociable, graceful and charming, refined and artistic and on the negative side — incapable of decision, unco-operative and dependent on others.

THE CENTRAL ISSUE THAT LIBRA NEEDS TO LEARN IS CO-OPERATION.

Spiritual development is brought about with and through relating harmoniously — harmonising and balancing ones own emotional needs with those of another effecting a creative compromise.

In the house of the zodiac where Libra rules the cusp is where you have been out of balance in previous lifetimes. You need to be adaptable with regard to the affairs of this house with a strong need to see both sides before any decision is made.

The evolution of the sign of Libra from undeveloped to developed is a journey from the negative qualities to the positive in the course of as many lives as it takes.

HOW DO I RELATE?

Undeveloped Librans have difficulty making choices because they seek approval from others and wish to please. The combination of depending on others for approval (instead of giving it to themselves) and idealising their mates and loved ones, thinking they are perfect, creates the problems which they ultimately learn from. Their tendency to idealise love also leads them to love themselves eventually and to see that love is not outside of them but comes from within.

Developed Librans are amicable, friendly, fair, tolerant, and the most advanced in social skills. They are pleasing to others without seeking only to please, co-operative and giving without giving themselves away, and tolerant of other points of view while having one of their own. Finally, they are their own person, capable of using their talents to support themselves in the world.

ASTROLOGY AND CRYSTALS

The Libra energy can be greatly assisted in its development by the use of the following crystals:

Howlite – This stone encourages balance between mental and physical levels.

Pink Tourmaline – stimulates harmony in relationship issues.

White Opal – for beauty, self-understanding and intuition.

FLOWER REMEDIES AND ASTROLOGY

The following are the Australian Bush Flower Essences that specifically assist the development of the Libra qualities to be expressed positively. They are however merely suggestions: -

Dog Rose —For improved self-confidence — for those who are shy.

Illawarra Flame Tree — for self approval or perceived rejection.

Red Grevillea — for being too reliant on others and for the courage to be who you are.

Rough Bluebell — For those who don't feel 'enough'.

ESSENTIAL OILS

Lavender, Spearmint, Peppermint, Fennel, Camomile.

ASTROLOGY AND THE TAROT

The tarot cards associated with the sign of Libra are: -

No. 3 The Empress, No. 8 Adjustment, The 2 of Swords, The 3 of Swords, The 4 of Swords.

No. 8 of the Major Arcana Adjustment. The coolness

of the air pervades the card. To be fair the masculine lady must be cool and free from emotions. The element air facilitates this. Adjustment is the art of balance — the scales are to weigh the pros and cons to arrive at a decision to take an action. The left brain logic is ever present and is offset by the blue green colours indicating a harmony and calm on inner levels and inner balance. The sword may indicate a mental clarity. The associated planet is Venus and it rules such things as beauty, love, relationships, art.

There is an air of perfection — the lady has to be always on her toes to constantly adjust herself to remain balanced.

Divinity is nothing more than perfect balance between harmony and disharmony.

THE SPIRITUAL LESSON OF LIBRA

The Libran spiritual lesson is about BROTHERHOOD. Brotherhood through relationships. Learning a deeper understanding of the law of equilibrium, which governs human life. Calls forth and tests the inner integrity of the soul. Learning to be their own inner light, to raise their mind above all conflict and find in their heart their own point of balance.

The number associated with Libra is the *NUMBER SIX*.

The keyword for the number six is *HARMONY*.

The number *SIX* has the qualities of love, harmony, justice and service to mankind. The life wants to be filled with love and meaningful relationships. Number six people realise the importance of love, compassion and social responsibility. Home also becomes part of the community in which law and order are established to ensure social harmony.

Positive keywords are:- love, understanding, guardianship, conscientiousness, service to mankind.

Negative keywords are:- anxiety, worry, bustling activity, mistaken ideals, unwilling service.

Some of the things that Libra rules are:- alliances, cosmetics, furniture, poetry and social affairs.

Libra people are happiest in careers involving partnerships and the adjusting of human relationships. They also need to work in pleasant surroundings. Some of the careers are diplomat, artist, interior decorators, attorneys, beauticians and hairdressers.

Countries ruled by Libra are :- Austria, Argentina, Burma, China, Tibet.

Cities are:- Antwerp, Copenhagen, Frankfurt, Leeds, Nottingham, Charleston.

Plants ruled by Libra are:- watercress, strawberry, violets, lemon thyme, pansy, primrose, white rose.

THE NEW UNITY CONSCIOUSNESS AND THE BALANCE OF THE POLARITIES.

As for all the polarities the key is in the bottom end (or internally). The top end is either a manifestation of the balance (success) or imbalance (dysfunction/failure). So "success" or "failure" depends on what is going on INSIDE. The outside world is merely a reflection of that.

So, the horoscope can be used to analyse what is causing the imbalance of a polarity and when you can actually name something and become conscious of it, it can then be resolved or healed. Using Astrology in this way is such a valuable tool to self-growth.

THE RELATIONSHIP AXIS

"There is one relationship that will always be there for you: your relationship to yourself." Kenneth Wydro.

The Relationship Axis is made up of the signs of Aries (which rules the First House) and Libra (which rules the Seventh House) which oppose each other (180 degrees) and the planets Mars and Venus. Mars is the masculine principle and Venus the feminine principle. You could extend this to the balance between the masculine and feminine within us (regardless of gender) or the 'inner marriage'.

The issue of this polarity is the balancing of the conflict between the self (Aries end) and the other (Libra end). The 'I' versus 'we'.

The point of unity is achieved when both ends of the polarity are integrated to a balance within the consciousness. Remember divinity is nothing more than the balance between opposites, which demystifies it and makes it possible for anyone to achieve. You have to understand and raise your consciousness to a 'point of balance'. Once this is achieved you cease to be the swinging pendulum, vulnerable to anything that 'throws you off-balance'.

This polarity must certainly be the most badly expressed of any of the six. As everyone knows, relating is something that human beings are bad at because they are refusing to KNOW WHO THEY REALLY ARE.

"Only when we have ourselves can we fully meet another human being without losing ourselves." Tracey Marks.

We need to experience all that is within us before we are ready to achieve a harmonious interaction with another. Be still (stop rushing about avoiding what is inside) and have the courage to experience your inner truth. When this is acknowledged you can then attend to your inner needs YOURSELF. Partners cannot do this for you!

"The doorway to others is through ourselves!" Tracey Marks.

It is usually that we don't (and don't want to) know ourselves that we seek another to get them to love that part of us (displayed by the Descendant point of the horoscope) that we don't own or like. This is the part of us that we perceive is not working well so we perceive that we need someone else to do these things for us. Eg: Leo Descendant could be interpreted that we don't feel socially confident so we would choose a partner that appears to have this confidence that we perceive we lack.

We need to be willing to experience conflict within ourselves and with others, while retaining the aim of peace, healing and resolution. Inner harmony is brought about because we are willing to confront problems and negotiate to have our needs met as well as meeting the needs of our partners.

The two issues of this polarity are: -

1. *PATIENCE* with ourselves in that our partners are only reflecting back to us pieces of ourselves that need redeeming.

2. *CO-OPERATION* in that we need to actively give consideration to meet the needs of both parties so win/win situations are created.

SCORPIO

I SEEK MYSELF THROUGH WHAT I DESIRE

Scorpio is ruled by the planet Pluto and before Pluto's discovery in 1930 by the planet Mars, which is the lower octave of Pluto. Scorpio rules the Eighth House of the zodiac and is opposite to Taurus, which rules the Second House. Scorpio is the top half of the VALUE AXIS.

Keywords for Scorpio are: -

Positive +: resourceful, intuitive, strong willed, secretive, transforming.

Negative -: destructive, vindictive, paranoid (secrecy), resentful, sarcastic.

The symbol for Scorpio is the eagle, the scorpion, or the phoenix. Scorpio is a water sign, which is of fixed expression.

Scorpio is the search for empowerment and the answer to life's secrets.

Physical rulership to parts of the body are — sex

organs, bladder, adenoids, nose, elimination of body wastes.

The general traits of the sign of Scorpio are on the positive side — powerful healing which is transformative, creative through re-building (rebirth), strong and loyal friend and on the negative side — destructive, seductive, misuse of power.

THE CENTRAL ISSUE THAT SCORPIO NEEDS TO LEARN IS FORGIVENESS.

Spiritual development is brought about through and with the understanding of the TRANSFORMATIONAL PROCESS OF LIFE — which is discovering the secrets of your own life.

In the house where Scorpio rules the cusp "deep involvement" is required. There is an emotional need for intense involvement and secrecy in order to fulfill subconscious needs. There will be an intense approach to the affairs of this house.

The evolution of the sign of Scorpio from undeveloped to developed is a journey from the negative qualities to the positive in the course of as many lives as it takes.

HOW DO I CHANGE?

The undeveloped Scorpio lifetimes are very painful and as they are stubborn and determined to have their way, power struggles are common. They are learning that their strength is in their vulnerability, not in having power over people and things. They find it difficult to forgive because they don't understand the part they play in the drama caused the situation. As a result of their experiences with love and loss, they develop insight into human nature and life's mysteries and learn to make more enlightened choices, which transform and empower instead of destroying. They need to understand that life is both uncontrollable and unpredictable and that they have the power to cope with whatever comes. So instead of trying to control life, they learn to master themselves by mastering their attitudes, therefore having self-mastery the ultimate power.

ASTROLOGY AND CRYSTALS

The Scorpio energy can be greatly assisted in its development by the use of the following crystals:

Black Opal – This stone is for transformation of repressed energy.

Obsidian — This stone is for emotional strength and self change.

Jet — This stone is for stored pain and it releases locked up feelings.

FLOWER REMEDIES AND ASTROLOGY.

The following are Australian Bush Flower Essences that assist in the positive expression of the Scorpio qualities. However they are merely suggestions.

Daggar Hakea — For resentment(s) and forgiveness.

Bush Iris — for stronger connection to your own spirit and also for the fear of death.

Billy Goat Plum — for Sexuality (balanced) and acceptance of the physical body.

ESSENTIAL OILS

Hycinth, Cardamom, Coffee (roasted seeds), Woodruff, Ylang Ylang.

ASTROLOGY AND THE TAROT

The tarot cards associated with the sign of Scorpio are: -

No. 13 Death (rebirth), Prince of Cups, 5 of Cups, 6 of Cups, 7 of Cups.

No. 13 of the Major Arcana Death. This card holds the 'secrets' of life itself — how to evolve and change. The never ending spiral of life (the whole Milky Way Galaxy is a giant spiral) the letting go of the old/past to make way for the new/future. This process happens whether it is voluntary or not! So you can have no pain or extreme pain — its your choice and that's whether you know it or not or even whether you like it or not. Scorpio, the sign of power for good or ill. Out of the destruction comes the rebirth and creation — the transformational process — the only constant in the universe is CHANGE. The scorpion is on the ground reacting, stinging, the phoenix is above in the air rising above earthly issues, the fish is about the middle of the card — the confusion in the 'middle' of the process. The webs and strings seem to be saying that we are all connected, be it indirectly or otherwise to the evolution of others. This card is an insight into the transformational process of life — in the physical sense the indestructibility of matter and science has proven that.

THE SPIRITUAL LESSON OF SCORPIO

The Scorpio spiritual lesson is about PEACE. Peace through spiritual vision. DEATH — to learn to LET GO so that change (death) can transform the old into birthing a new vision for the future.

The number associated with Scorpio is the NUMBER SEVEN.

The keyword for the number seven is ANALYSIS.

Seven goes within itself to contemplate its place in the universe. It begins to think and to analyse past experiences and present situations, and it wonders what lies ahead. Seven realises that the skills it has developed must be perfected in preparation for the future. Seven is physical rest and metal work.

Positive keywords are :- technicality, trust, poise, introspection, silence.

Negative keywords are;- melancholy, sarcasm, skepticism, malice, faithlessness.

Some of the things that Scorpio rules are:- bathrooms, espionage, funerals, taxes and laboratories.

Scorpio people enjoy "impossible" tasks. They like work, which demands determined effort and intense concentration. Work connected with the underground or liquids or sanitation also appeal. Some of the careers are detectives, morticians, politicians, chemists, surgeons, dentists, scientists, archaeologists and garbage collectors.

Countries ruled by Scorpio are: – Norway, Catalonia, Mauritania, Parts of Germany, Sardinia, Morocco, Algeria, Syria, Lybia and Egypt.

Peoples ruled by Scorpio are the Arab people.

Plants ruled by Scorpio are: – bramble, horehound, leek, wormwood, blackthorn, blackberry leaves.

UNITY CONSCIOUSNESS AND THE BALANCE OF THE POLARITIES.

THE VALUE AXIS

"Courage means the power to LET GO of the familiar and the secure." Rollo May.

The Value Axis is made up of the signs of Taurus (which rules the Second House) and Scorpio (which rules the Eighth House) which oppose each other (180 degrees) and the planets Venus and Pluto. Venus rules values (self value) and Pluto rules power or the lack of. No self value = no power. Simple. There is no more to it than that.

"The root of all evil: lack of love for yourself". Unknown.

The issue of this polarity is the balancing of the conflict between the gaining of power authentically Vs gaining it externally. This is simple too — any power gained externally is addiction, not power, it only looks that way!

When we are insecure inside, the greater the need to gain security from others and things. When YOU are enough then it doesn't matter what others do or don't do, you will handle it.

When you are enough, you always have enough. When you perceive you aren't enough, no amount is ever enough.

So to possess ourselves gives us the freedom to detach and feel worthy enough to want the very best for ourselves and that we don't need to hoard or fear lack and that sharing brings more to us.

We are all worthy just because we are born.

When we are secure inside and have good self esteem and self worth levels our value systems are very different to when we are perceiving that we are unworthy and insecure.

SAGITTARIUS

I SEEK THEREFORE I AM

Sagittarius is ruled by the planet Jupiter and also rules the Ninth House of the zodiac. Sagittarius is the sign opposite Gemini which rules the Third House. Sagittarius is the top half of the KNOWLEDGE AXIS.

Keywords for Sagittarius are: -

Positive +: expansive, far-seeing, truth revealing, adventurous, generous.

Negative -: exaggerating, self-righteous, coarse, tactless, boastful.

The symbol for Sagittarius is the Centaur shooting an arrow into the sky. Sagittarius is a fire sign of mutable expression.

Sagittarius is the search for the TRUTH and WISDOM using the higher mind faculties.

The physical rulership to parts of the body are — hips, thighs, muscles, sciatic nerve (hip nerve) and the motor nerve action.

The general traits of the sign of Sagittarius are on the positive side — vast and inspirational mind, sees the larger issue, magnanimous and generous, and on the negative side — loud mouthed and coarse, dictator and propagandist, tends to false exaggerations.

THE CENTRAL ISSUE THAT SAGITTARIUS NEEDS TO LEARN IS RESTRAINT.

Spiritual development is brought about with and through the search for truth and wisdom and the stimulation of the *HIGHER MIND.*

In the house where Sagittarius rules the cusp is where you need to expand your experiences. You have felt limited in the affairs of this house in previous lifetimes, so you need to explore all the areas of that house. Don't over-expand.

The evolution of the sign of Sagittarius from undeveloped to developed is a journey from the negative qualities to the positive in the course of as many lives as it takes.

HOW FAR DO I GO?

The undeveloped Sagittarian lifetimes are spent wandering aimlessly and/or alone in the "wilderness". This over indulgence in wandering and not having any demands of life put on them, gives the Sagittarian a false view of life, where they think its just one long free ride. What they need to learn is that every person's life has a meaning or purpose to it, in an evolutionary sense, and they need to discover theirs and then put that into a wider context to also mean something in the grand scheme of things. Sagittarians lack sensitivity and tend to be gross regardless of gender, due to the amount of time spent in independent exploration of life, and not paying attention to the feelings of others.

Probably due to the overemphasis of freedom in the early lives, the developed Sagittarian is wise as a result of all their adventures and travelling, in a philosophical and cultural sense. The developed Sagittarian has an all-encompassing philosophy that allows limitless expansion of thought into the Higher Mind so eternal Higher Learning is allowed.

ASTROLOGY AND CRYSTALS

The Sagittarian energy can be greatly assisted in its

development by the use of the following crystals:

Sodalite — This stone aids mental balance, clear thinking, widens perspective.

Turquoise — This stone is for luck, healing and wisdom. Turquoise is called the traveller's stone as it protects the wearer.

Topaz — This stone is for flexibility, strength and balance and working with the Higher Mind.

FLOWER REMEDIES AND ASTROLOGY

The following are Australian Bush Flower Essences that facilitate the positive qualities of the sign of Sagittarius to be expressed. They are however merely suggestions.

Green Spider Orchid — To not blab secrets or for foot-in-mouth disease.

Freshwater Mangrove — This flower is for expansion of consciousness. It also allows the person to embrace a wider scope of possibilities where the belief system is more 'open-ended' for the highest good of all.

Angelsword — This flower is for communication to the

Higher Self/Mind and for spiritual discrimination.

ESSENTIAL OILS

Saffron, Sage, Nutmeg, Bergamot, Clove, Oakmoss (lichen).

ASTROLOGY AND THE TAROT

The tarot cards associated with the sign of Sagittarius are: -

No. 10 Fortune, No. 14 Art, Princess of Wands, Knight of Wands, 2 of Disks, 4 of Swords, 6 of Wands, 8 of Wands, 9 of Cups, 9 of Wands.

No. 14 of the Major Arcana Art. Sagittarius is the sign of the Higher Mind so the integration of opposites in this card may mean to make one whole and therefore operating on higher levels. Sagittarius also rules metaphysics (meta= beyond and physics = the physical) so this process of integration constantly throughout the card eg: right brain with left brain etc. would enable the querent to go beyond the physical to higher realms (to higher frequencies of ourselves) a creative quantam leap to higher insights. The name of the card "Art" could mean the art of alchemy, or transformation of trivia/data (Gemini) to meaning (Sagittarius). It is significant that you must go inward with this card to achieve this end, so within each of us we have the power to create energy for the highest good of all.

The association of Jupiter with this card would also indicate a general benevolent understanding of higher truths, allowing tolerence of differences.

GROWTH – EXPANSION- PROGRESS.

THE SPIRITUAL LESSON OF SAGITTARIUS.

The Sagittarian spiritual lesson is about *LOVE*. Love through communication – learning to understand the immense power of thought and to communicate this understanding to their fellow man.

The number associated with Sagittarius is the **NUMBER THREE.**

The keyword for the number three is *EXPANSION.*

This number is also associated with the sign of Gemini so please see the notes contained there.

Some of the things that Sagittarius rules are: -

alters, archery, dreams, foreign affairs, and travel.

Sagittarian people like any work where foresight and a willingness to take a chance is offered. Some of the careers are – psychiatrists, law, veterinarians, ministers, interpreters, explorers, librarians, professional sports, and travel occupations.

Countries ruled by Sagittarius are:- Hungary, Spain, Dalmatia, ancient Crete and Madagascar.

Cities ruled by Sagittarius are:- Avignon, Cologne, Toledo, Stuttgart, Budapest, York and Nottingham.

Plants ruled by Sagittarius are:- horsetail, feverfew, agrimony and mallows.

UNITY CONSCIOUSNESS AND THE BALANCE OF POLARITIES.

THE KNOWLEDGE AXIS

"We shall not cease from exploration and the end of all our exploring will be to arrive at where we started and know the place for the first time." T. S. ELIOT.

The Knowledge Axis is made up of the signs of Gemini

(which rules the Third House) and Sagittarius (which rules the Ninth House) which oppose each other (180 degrees) and the ruling planets Mercury and Jupiter.

Mercury rules communication, data, facts etc. (Gemini) and Jupiter rules expansion, metaphysics, wisdom (Sagittarius)

The issue of this polarity is that TRUTH AND MEANING are always within you, not in some far off land or in reading libraries of books.

Developing a philosophy or belief system for your life (Sag) depends on what information is gathered (Gemini). A belief system that doesn't allow new information into it because the information doesn't align with it is a flawed one.

Keep your belief systems flexible, so as new information comes to hand and new things are learned, they can be incorporated into your beliefs or philosophy to allow you to live truthfully.

When learning is 'blocked' there is no opportunity for expansion/growth/evolution. Wisdom (Sag) is gained by gathering all the data (Gemini) to a focal point of meaning (Sag) to access the truth.

The doorway to 'higher' isn't up or out, it's IN to experience the upward spiral of the higher frequencies of ourselves and life.

CAPRICORN

I SEEK MYSELF THROUGH WHAT I USE

Capricorn is ruled by the planet Saturn and rules the Tenth House of the zodiac. Capricorn is the sign opposite Cancer, which rules the Fourth House. Capricorn is the top half of the SECURITY AXIS.

Keywords for Capricorn are:-

Positive +: achieving, structuring, conservative, responsible, ambitious.

Negative-: stiff, denying, worried, competitive, restricting.

The symbol for Capricorn is the Goat with a dolphin's tail.

Capricorn is the search for achievement, goals and success and in the journey towards these things maturity is gained.

The physical rulership to parts of the body are — knees, joints, skin, gall bladder, chilling and cold.

The general traits of Capricorn are on the positive

side — Organising and executive abilities, prudent and self-sacrificing, aware of other peoples needs, and on the negative side — miserly and demanding, unsympathetic and secretive and worships only position and prestige.

THE CENTRAL ISSUE THAT CAPRICORN NEEDS TO LEARN IS SOCIAL-ABILITY AND RESPONSE-ABILITY

Spiritual development is brought about by the right use of their authority and social power for the highest good of all NOT for their individual benefit.

In the house where Capricorn rules the cusp is where we need respect and recognition from others, but do not actively pursue this recognition for it can only be earned through merit. There is always a feeling of frustration with regard to the affairs of the house ruled by Capricorn (Saturn).

The evolution of the sign of Capricorn from undeveloped to developed is a journey from the negative qualities to the positive in the course of as many lives as it takes.

WHAT IS MY SOCIAL ROLE?

Undeveloped Capricorns tend to be greedy and selfish as they aren't connected to their emotional feeling self. This disconnection to the feelings makes them insecure emotionally so they compensate with positions of 'power' and material gain. So their lives are very 'business like' and cold, the lonely executive at the top of the tower who drives an expensive car, but goes home to an empty space. In the early lifetimes Capricorns are developing the qualities of reponse — ability, reliability, practicality, and endurance, which many of them acquire from literally attending to business. Capricorns are driven and ambitious, and are learning to handle authority and to face ethical issues and morals. Getting what they want by expressing cold ruthlessness is not the way to go.

The developed Capricorns have the ability to provide for themselves and others, and to also teach others how they can achieve. The well-balanced Capricorn is powerful and is master not only over themselves, but also life's laws, building both social structures and the actual structures. So once Capricorns have climbed the corporate ladder, they often use their elevated social positions to make changes that will improve society.

ASTROLOGY AND CRYSTALS

Dumortierite:- This stone is for discipline and organisation.

Ruby:- Ruby attracts empowerment and leadership and the confidence to do it.

Black Tourmaline:- This stone is for concentration and self discipline.

FLOWER REMEDIES AND ASTROLOGY

The following are Australian Bush Flower Essences that specifically assist the development of the Capricorn qualities to be expressed positively.

Sunshine Wattle:- for the overly serious or for those prone to depression.

Boab:- This bush flower essence is for the breaking of family patterns of fear driven emotions.

Little Flannel Flower - For grimness, pessimism and negativity.

ESSENTIAL OILS

Cypress, Patchouly, Myrrh, Honeysuckle, Vertivert, Lilac.

ASTROLOGY AND THE TAROT

The tarot cards associated with the sign of Capricorn are:- No. 15 The Devil, No. 21 The Universe, The Queen of Disks, 4 of Disks, 5 of Wands, 7 of Disks, 10 of Wands.

No. 15 of the Major Arcarna The Devil. This card feels as though things really aren't as they seem. Capricorn energy would indicate ambitions, but the motives of yourself and/or others may be deceptive. Examine the motivations to get to the real reasons for your actions — if negative or destructive then some changes may need to be made.

Creative energy is great, just be sure of what it is or you may create something you don't want! The opposite polarity of Capricorn is Cancer, so make sure it isn't some negative phobia/fear that is driving you on, or some emotional fear.

This card is also about projections — those disowned

characteristics of ourselves that we refuse to recognise. Power comes from wisdom, not fears. Wisdom and power are also achieved through the process of hard knocks or failure (7 of Disks) and disappointments, to show responsibility and organisation/determination, and directing our will in a focused manner leads to success. This card is about the physical side of life and another keyword for it is *EGO*. The words out of the Lord's Prayer "lead us not into temptation and deliver us from evil" apply to this card.

THE CAPRICORN SPIRITUAL LESSON

is about *SERVICE. SERVICE IN ACTION.* Learning to become strong enough to dissolve all crystalisation of the lower self (ego). Overcoming self centredness and selfishness, learning responsibility for humanity.

ASTROLOGY AND NUMEROLOGY

The number associated with Capricorn is the *NUMBER EIGHT*.

The keyword for the number eight is *REWARD*.

This number is very karmic where the Eight reaps what it has sown. All the strength and skill gathered in the past seven numbers are put to the test. The rewards for its past efforts come in equal proportion to the wisdom of past choices. The Eight person is the executive type who has organisational and managerial abilities and has self-empowerment.

So as a person that is in a position of authority you must accept responsibility and handle it fairly because your actions have obvious repercussions in the world around you. As a steward of material resources, you must handle them wisely and with respect.

Some of the things that Capricorn rules are:- cement, government, ice, mathematics, mountains and Saturday.

Capricorns are happiest in careers calling for organising ability, integrity, and perserverance. Some careers are mathematics, civil servants, osteopaths, politicians, public administration, government service, accountancy, financial advisors, or a career in banking.

Countries ruled by Capricorn are:- Albania, Lithuania, Bulgaria, Afganistan, Mexico and India.

Cities are:- Oxford, Brussels, Port Said, Delhi.

Peoples are: the Hindu's.

Plants ruled by Capricorn are:- Wintergreen for rheumatism in the joints, Comfrey for bones, sometimes called "knitbone". Hemlock, black poppy.

UNITY CONSCIOUSNESS AND THE BALANCE OF POLARITIES.

THE SECURITY AXIS

"Learning how to make others trust you is the best protection there is, and it will make you safer than all the armor you can find." MERLE SHAIN.

The Security Axis is made up of the signs of Cancer (which rules the Fourth House) and Capricorn (which rules the Tenth House) which oppose each other (180 degrees) and the ruling planets of The Moon and Saturn.

The Moon rules emotions, family, the feminine principle, nurturance (Cancer) and Saturn rules restriction, karma, fears.

The issue of this polarity is INNER security and self mastery over family dysfunctional patterns to become emotionally self-sufficient.

Whether we had a "bad" or "good" family experience

as a child has an affect on whether we can become a "success" in the outside world. There have been many who had a "bad" childhood and made good, and many who had a "good" childhood and didn't find success. So, its not so much what happens to us, but how we handle what happens to us that matters.

When we learn to parent ourselves (Cancer), we can then take our place in the world (Capricorn).

However, there are many "adult children" who didn't mature and take on the responsibility to nurture themselves and achieve their ambitions and goals.

The balance of this polarity is achieved by taking a personal responsibility to heal your own emotional wounds, giving yourself the necessary strength to achieve your goals.

To integrate the Cancer/Capricorn polarity, emotional security is the key factor, as success in the outside world needs to be sustained by the connection to the feeling world, which is nourished in the home and family environment.

AQUARIUS

I SEEK MYSELF THROUGH HUMANITY

Aquarius is ruled by the unusual planet Uranus and also rules the Eleventh House of the zodiac. Aquarius is the sign opposite Leo, which rules the Fifth House. Aquarius is the top half of the CREATIVITY AXIS. The bottom half (Leo) is personal creativity and the top half (Aquarius) is cultural creativity.

Keywords for Aquarius are: -

Positive +: insightful, innovative, original, friendly, broadminded.

Negative -: know-it-all, disrupting, rebellious, perverse, aloof.

The symbol for Aquarius is the Waterbearer or Man pouring water on the earth. The water is symbolic of enlightenment being poured on the earthplane. Aquarius is an air sign and is of a fixed quality.

Aquarius is the search for 'the group' and social relationships. The sign is symbolic (the glyph) of the dissemination of information.

Physical rulership to parts of the body are — the retina of the eye, calves of the legs, ankles, electricity of the body, blood circulation, anaemia, elimination of carbon dioxide through breathing.

The general traits of Aquarius are on the positive side — gregarious and social, strives for brotherhood, loyalty to a cause or idea, and on the negative side — tries to impose own ideas on others, have zany schemes that are impractical.

THE CENTRAL CORE ISSUE THAT AQUARIUS NEEDS TO LEARN IS WARMTH.

Spiritual development is brought about through and with contributing to the highest good of the group or collective (social reform).

In the house where Aquarius rules the cusp is where you need to obtain new knowledge in order to breakdown old ideals from past lifetimes.

The evolution of the sign of Aquarius from undeveloped to developed is a journey from the negative qualities to the positive in the course of as many lives as it *takes.*

HOW CAN I MAKE A DIFFERENCE?

Undeveloped Aquarians tend to be shy and distant, not connecting to their destined role. This role is destined by themselves and isn't dumped on them 'from a great height', but is the expression of their ideal for the collective. The undeveloped Aquarian may also have an ego problem, which prevents them from perceiving themselves as equal to others in the group, therefore being superior and knowing-it-all.

The developed Aquarian is inventive and creative (with an open heart-centre), with many ideals for improvements to social and scientific areas. Although they don't 'shine' in one-on-one relationships they make great friends and flourish in relationships that allow them freedom to be the unique individuals they are. Aquarians have huge potential in presenting progressive ideas to pave the way for future progress and improvements to the human condition and social reforms.

ASTROLOGY AND CRYSTALS

The Aquarian energy can be greatly assisted in its

development by the use of the following crystals.

The classic Aquarian stone is Lapis Lazuli – This stone is for friendship, self-discipline, psychic abilities, and to open the throat and third eye chakras.

Aquamarine – purifies and calms through acceptance of self, also good for fluid retention.

Milky Quartz – this stone is for understanding and integration of multi-levels of psychic growth.

ASTROLOGY AND FLOWER REMEDIES

The following are Australian Bush Flower Essences that specifically assist the development of the Aquarian qualities to be expressed positively. However they are merely suggestions.

Tall Yellow Top – this essence is for loneliness and isolation and for when there is a sense of abandonment.

Flannel Flower – for being distant emotionally and disconnected to the feeling nature.

Tall Mulla Mulla – for the encouragement of social interaction, or where there are fears of confrontation.

ESSENTIAL OILS

Lavender, Patchouly, Lemon Verbena, Parsley, Pine, Sweet Pea.

ASTROLOGY AND THE TAROT

The tarot cards associated with the sign of Aquarius are:- No. 0 The Fool, No. 17 The Star Card, The Prince of Swords, 7 of Swords, 6 of Swords, 5 of Swords.

No. 17 The Star Card. This card is the card of HOPE and is saying that emotional detachment and coolness (cool colours) enable the universal lifeforce energy to flow through you, making you a channel for the highest good of all. The star is emanating energy in a spiral out-pouring into the universe, beckoning mankind to look upward towards new visions for the future.

This is a very futuristic card, the Aquarian association is to do with humanitarian issues — the naked lady symbolises the natural beauty of all, the sensuality. The large earth sphere in the background seems to be saying — earthlings — people need to relate to the cosmos and Earth's place in the grand scheme of things.

Nurturing the individual no matter how different or alien — everything is inter-related-oneness. Protecting the Earth; ecology.

Ideas, ideals, humanitarian concerns, hope for the future, visions.

The Aquarian spiritual lesson is about BROTHERHOOD. Universal Brotherhood — learning to work with the Uranian energy to realease the solid Saturnian nature to Spiritual Truth. Becoming as one with all mankind.

ASTROLOGY AND NUMEROLOGY

The numbers associated with Aquarius and the planet Uranus (The Awakener) are the NUMBER NINE and also the NUMBER ELEVEN.

The keyword for the number nine is RELEASE.

In its best expression 9 is the humanitarian number carrying light and wisdom. The 9 people's power is in their understanding of human nature. They can often be found doing work of a humanitarian nature. The 9 must learn to have no expectations of reward, if this is genuine then reward sometimes comes for all — not just that individual.

The keyword for number eleven 11 is the *SPIRITUAL MESSENGER*.

The 11 persons power is in their intuition, so they deliver messages of inspiration to others..

Some of the things that Aquarius rules are:- Astrology, aviation, electricity, gases, inventions and the wireless or radio.

Aquarian people like any work which allows scope for inventiveness and the detached application of special rules, and formulae. Some of the careers are scientists, inventors, radiologists, photographers, radio and TV, radio operators, civil service, electricians, lecturing and public corporations as well as the social sciences.

Countries ruled by Aquarius are; - Sweden, Ethiopia, Prussia, Russia, Lithuania, Westphalia, Canada, Parts of Arabia and Poland.

Cities are: - Hamburg, Saltzburg, Trent, Stockholm and Lenningrad.

Plants ruled by Aquarius are:- Frankincense and Myrrh.

UNITY CONSCIOUSNESS AND THE BALANCE OF POLARITIES.

THE CREATIVITY AXIS

"True equality can only mean the right to be uniquely creative." Milton Erickson.

The Creativity Axis is made up of the signs of Leo (which rules the Fifth House) and Aquarius (which rules the Eleventh House) which oppose each other (180 degrees) and the ruling planets of The Sun and Uranus.

The Sun rules our identity, the masculine principle, the spirit (Leo) and Uranus rules humanity or the Group/Society.

The issue of this polarity is the connection to the HEART CENTRE so the spirit may flow freely and contribute to the collective for the highest good of all.

When our heart centre is open and flowing well (unobstructed) we are an open portal for the universal love energy to pour into our lives. If the heart centre is closed/blocked or not flowing then joy, abundance and creativity are also blocked.

LOVE IS THE CREATIVE ENERGY.

The Leo end is the individual creativity (or one-on-one love) and the Aquarius end is the cultural creativity.

The love for self (not ego inspired) can then be radiated to humanity through groups and friends and associations into the collective.

When we learn to fully express who we are through an open heart chakra, then we are able to contribute our unique gifts and talents to the collective to add to the pool of cultural creativity.

So when we appreciate our unique and different abilities we can also love the differences of others, embracing the collective through the experience of our own self-love and open-hearted way of being that the ego cannot inhibit.

PISCES

I SEEK MYSELF THROUGH UNIVERSAL UNDERSTANDING

"If I have told you earthly things and ye believe not, how shall ye believe if I tell you of heavenly things?" John 3:12.

Pisces is ruled by the planet Neptune (before 1846 Jupiter) and also rules the Twelfth House of the zodiac. Pisces is the sign opposite Virgo, which rules the Sixth House. Pisces is the top half of the UNDERSTANDING AXIS.

Keywords for Pisces are:-

Positive+: compassionate, sympathetic, imaginative, idealistic, giving.

Negative-: escapist, impractical, self-deceiving, illusory, over-sensitive.

The symbol for Pisces is the two fishes tied together, swimming in opposite directions. Pisces is a water sign of mutable expression.

Pisces is the search for FAITH in a world filled

with FEAR. Fear being something that prevents you from having faith and separating you from the whole (infinity or the all-that-is).

The physical rulership to parts of the body are — the feet, toes, lymph glands, sweat glands and mucus secretions.

The general traits of Pisces are on the positive side — natural tendency to vast imagination, understanding and compassion, and on the negative side — poor sense of individuality, hallucinatory and paranoid.

THE CENTRAL CORE ISSUE THAT PISCES NEEDS TO LEARN IS PERSEVERANCE.

Spiritual development is brought about with and through frustrations, atonements, service and ultimate understanding of the God within.

In the house where Pisces rules the cusp is where you need to allow your intuition to guide you for you will feel as though you are acting blindly.

The evolution of the sign of Pisces from undeveloped to developed is a journey from the negative qualities to the positive in the course of as many lives as it takes.

HOW DO I BECOME COMPASSIONATE?

The undeveloped Piscean must learn to move from self pity, indecision and feelings of inadequacy (which sometimes leads to the escapism of alcoholism, drugs or daydreaming) to practical uses of imagination and the idealism in the arts — acting —selfless service and healing. Undeveloped Pisceans have difficulty accepting and dealing with reality. Life is a deep disappointment and a rude joke to many Pisceans, leaving them deeply sad and depressed.

They need to acknowledge their sensitivity, learn to value their visions without getting lost in them, and channel their creativity and intuition constructively. They must also accept the responsibilities of being alive, and as they evolve, their ability to be more practical (Virgo end) allows them to be more in the moment and so be more grounded.

Pisceans are here to serve. Through service (Virgo end) they find a sense of belonging, in that they are communicators of the world of the spirit to others less attuned to it. The evolved Piscean understands the spiritual side of life and they can guide others to an understanding of the nature of the universe. They are the mystics and the healers of the spirit.

ASTROLOGY AND CRYSTALS

The Piscean energy can be greatly assisted in its development by the use of the following crystals.

The classic Piscean stone is the Amethyst — reduces negativity and encourages a connection to the spirit.

Sapphire — for a calm and inner peace and meditation.

Blue Tourmaline — for imagination and dreamwork.

ASTROLOGY AND FLOWER REMEDIES

The following are Australian Bush Flower Essences that specifically assist the development of the Picean qualities to be expressed positively. However, they are merely suggestions.

Fringed Violet — for psychic protection, seals the aura and heals any holes in it.

Sundew — for grounding to offset vagueness, keeps you "here". Being in the present moment is (KNOWING, while you are *NOWING* you are *KNOWING*. The *NOW* moment is your point of power.

Silver Princess — for the "swimming in the ocean of non-achievement" or drifting, gives direction.

ESSENTIAL OILS

Sandalwood, Vanilla, Frankincense, Myrrh, Camphor and Jasmine.

ASTROLOGY AND THE TAROT

The tarot cards associated with the sign of Pisces are: - The Priestess, The Hanged Man, The Moon, The Princess of Cups, 8 of Cups, 9 of Cups, 10 of Cups.

The Moon card relates to the Twelfth House and the sign of Pisces. There are wisps of mist or shrouds of filmy colour all over the card symbolising the vague/illusory/nebulous nature of the card — illusion and delusion. The line drawn across the card has something to do with the inaccessible reaches of reality, for e.g. the subconscious, or dreams in the night where it is difficult to 'see' clearly. Old cycles and patterns are held here underlying our conscious mind in the dark recesses of our memory. So this card is very much magnetic, receptive, PASSIVE or feminine in nature. Because the Moon rules the past this card is relating to karma and karmic patterns/habits: the burning off of karma or the struggle with the subconscious. The plunging of the depths in the hope of new levels of consciousness.

Illusion, fluctuations, deception, dreaminess, confusion.

The Piscean spiritual lesson is about PEACE. Peace – inner peace. To learn to control the restless emotions, and to become calm in spirit. Be still and know you are God.

ASTROLOGY AND NUMEROLOGY

The number associated with Pisces and the Planet Neptune (the Dissolver) is the NUMBER THIRTY THREE 33.

33 is the number of SPIRITUAL MASTERY, selfless service and universal understanding. The ability to 'rise above' life's dilemmas. This is the one who has mastery over the self – where there is a lapse in this self mastery then they lapse back into the negative

qualities of the 6 where they crave love, friends, and the domestic environment and there is no acceptance of their circumstances.

Some of the things that Pisces rules are: - anesthetics, drugs, hospitals, clouds, the metaphysical world, and institutions and shut-away places of isolation.

Piscean people enjoy and are found in many different occupations, but most of them would enjoy work connected with animals, films, footwear, or the sea. Some of the careers are, musicians, magicians, doctors, actors, artists, poets, nurses, prison attendants, asylum attendants, psychiatrists, social workers and teachers.

Countries ruled by Pisces are: - Portugal, Normandy, Upper Egypt (Nubia), Northern Spain, and Calabria.

Plants ruled by Pisces are — seaweeds, ferns, mosses, water lily, and all other plants which grow in water.

Cities are : - Alexandria, Seville, Worms, Lancaster, and Compostella.

UNITY CONSCIOUSNESS AND THE

BALANCE OF POLARITIES

THE UNDERSTANDING AXIS

"What you believe is true for you, so be very careful of what you believe because its creating your reality"
Helen Adams.

The Understanding Axis is made up of the signs of Virgo (which rules the Sixth House) and Pisces (which rules the Twelfth House) which oppose each other (180 degrees) and the ruling planets of Mercury and Neptune.

The planet Mercury rules the thinking processes and attitudes and the intellect (Virgo) and Neptune rules the world of spirit and illusion (Pisces).

The issue of the polarity is the connection to our SPIRITUAL NATURE and universal understanding, therefore allowing us to have compassion and unconditional love. There is a constant polarisation between fear and faith. Therefore our task is to unify and balance this polarisation so we are ONE WITH THE ALL-THAT-IS.

The Virgo end (sixth house) of this polarity when

dysfunctional is intolerant and does not accept things the way they are. The overly fussy Virgo is always pre-occupied with perfection, which of course can't be reached, causing anxiety. So there must be acceptance of the self first, and then tolerance of others, to facilitate compassion and universal understanding.

Acceptance is necessary to facilitate healing. Without the acceptance there is continual "fighting against" something, which does not allow healing.

To heal you must first accept the undesirable disease (whatever it is), and then have the intention of understanding how it was created, and for what reason. It is in the healing of ourselves that we become a healing force for others — hence the term "The Wounded Healer". It is by going into the wound that the healing happens.

So discrimination needs to be used to know when things are healing or harming.

There needs to be a wholistic approach to healing which involves understanding (Pisces) the relationship between mind, spirit, feelings and body.

CHAPTER 2 - THE SUN

The Sun represents our inner light, which seeks to illuminate us as to the purpose of our physical life.

By using the houses of the zodiac as a clock, with each house being a 2 hour division of the 24 hour long day, we can get an important insight into how our identity can be expressed.

The Sun is placed in the house by the TIME OF BIRTH, so if you were born at 3am, then your Sun would sit in the 2nd house, which is ruled by the sign Taurus and the planet Venus. So no matter what sun sign your birthday is in, your Sun will still have a TAURUS OVERLAY, because it is placed in the 2nd house which is the division of the zodiac between the hours of 2am and 4am.

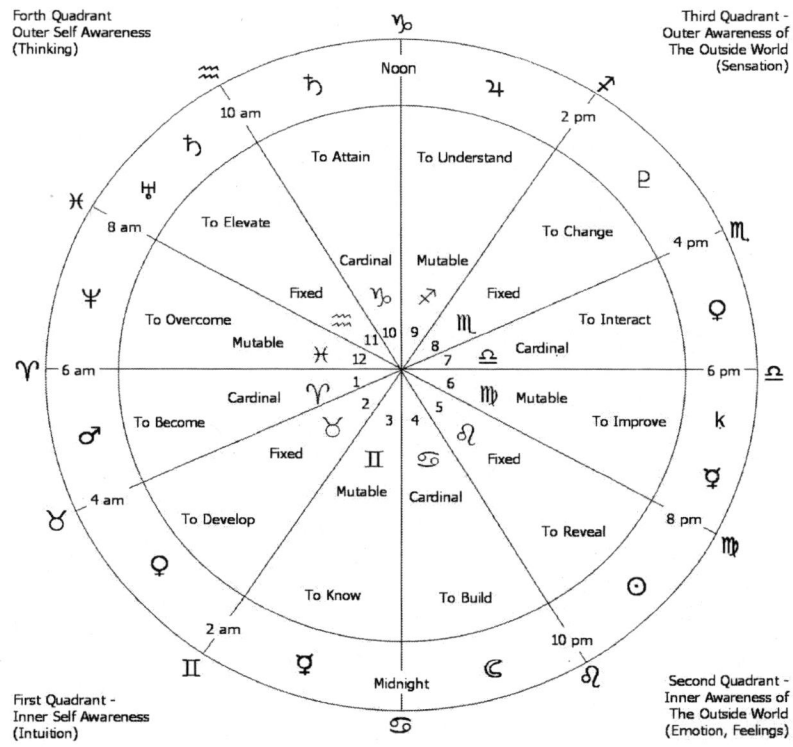

Below are the meanings for all the 12 houses and times of the zodiac.

<u>**The First House / 4 am – 6 am:-**</u>

This house is ruled by Aries ♈ and Mars ♂.

Aries is the drop out of the vast ocean (♓) into individuality and how to BECOME. Becoming the SELF through the courage to be self-aware and take action accordingly, to be self-determining. TO BE OR NOT TO BE – that is the quest! There is the issue here of whether the SELF is strong enough to stop running and rushing and actually have the courage to BE STILL AND KNOW self or not.

The Australian Bush Flower Remedy – Black Eyed Susan helps for these matters.

The issue for this house is PATIENCE.

The Second House / 2am – 4am:-

This house is ruled by Taurus ♉ and Venus ♀.

Taurus is about the desire to DEVELOP a sense of self worth through the experience of earning money by expressing talents and values. Inner security is developed with these experiences that make tangible your perception of your self-value.

The Australian Bush Flower Remedy that helps with these matters is – Five Corners.

The issue for this house is DETACHMENT.

The Third House / Midnight – 2am:-

This house is ruled by Gemini ♊ and Mercury ♀.

Gemini is about the desire to KNOW and begin to understand through knowledge and information. These people enjoy relating this knowledge through learning, teaching, networking and communicating to the community in some way.

The Australian Bush Flower Remedy that helps

with these matters is – Jacaranda

The issue for this house is MENTAL FOCUS.

The Fourth House / 10pm – Midnight:-

This house is ruled by Cancer ♋ and the Moon ☾.

Cancer is all about the desire to BUILD strong emotional foundations on which to construct your life. Emotional security is built through the domestic environment with the family and experiences with the mother or being a parent.

The Australian Bush Flower Remedy that helps with this is – Bottlebrush.

The issue for this house is EMOTIONAL SECURITY.

The Fifth House / 8pm – 10pm:-

This house is ruled by Leo ♌ and the Sun ☉.

Leo is about the desire to REVEAL their creativity and express their identity through the heart centre with love, as the person is centred in their integrity. When creativity is revealed through the heart the ego is balanced and there is no need to dominate. The Leo creative self-expression gives great enjoyment and happiness to the self and others by their sunny disposition.

The Australian Bush Flower Remedy that helps

with this is – Bluebell.

The issue for this house is HUMILITY.

The Sixth House / 6pm – 8pm:-

This house is ruled by Virgo ♍ and Chiron ⚷ (Co- ruler Mercury ☿).

Virgo is about the desire to IMPROVE relations with yourself and others by HEALING your life and gaining an understanding of the causes of dis-ease through the experiences of health, work (daily routine) and service. There will be experiences that invite the person to accept *what is* before healing happens.

The Australian Bush Flower Remedy that helps with this is – Yellow Cowslip Orchid.

The issue for this house is TOLERANCE.

The Seventh House / 4pm – 6pm:-

This house is ruled by Libra ♎ and Venus ♀.

Libra is about the desire to INTERACT with others in a "we" (♎) not "me" (♈) basis. Becoming aware of others and how to interact harmoniously in marriage and all relationships comes when the art of compromise is learned to bring about constant win/win situations.

The Australian Bush Flower Remedy that helps

with this is – Kangaroo Paw.

The issue for this house is CO-OPERATION.

The Eighth House / 2pm – 4pm:-

This house is ruled by Scorpio ♏ and Pluto ♇. Scorpio is about the desire for POWER. However, this empowerment doesn't happen until the ego is willing to concede that there is a need to change, and will allow the transformation through sharing of personal resources and intimacy (trust). It must be understood that resistance to change is disempowering and weakens the spritual connection.

The Australian Bush Flower Remedy that helps with this is – Bush Iris.

The issue for this house is FORGIVENESS.

The Ninth House / Midday – 2pm:-

This house is ruled by Sagittarius ♐ and Jupiter ♃. Sagittarius is about seeking the truth and the use of the Higher Mind to gain wisdom and UNDERSTANDING. There will be experiences that invite a broadening of the belief system through travel, philosophy, foreign cultures and HIGHER learning.

The Australian Bush Flower Remedy that helps with this is – Freshwater Mangrove.

The issue for this house is WISDOM.

The Tenth House / 10am – Midday:-

This house is ruled by Capricorn ♑ and Saturn ♄. Capricorn is about achieving success, and in this journey towards social recognition, maturity is gained. This maturity allows the person to be response-able. Social status has with it the responsibility to work toward the benefits of others.

The Australian Bush Flower Remedy that helps with this is – Southern Cross.

The issue for this house is SOCIAL ABILITY.

The Eleventh House / 8am – 10am:-

This house is ruled by Aquarius ♒ and Uranus ♅. Aquarius is about new and innovative ideas that would be of benefit for the group. Experiences that ELEVATE the consciousness are with friends, groups and social interactions regarding humanitarian concerns.

The Australian Bush Flower Remedy that helps with this is – Slender Rice Flower.

The issue for this house is WARMTH FROM THE HEART.

The Twelfth House / 6am – 8am:-

This house is ruled by Pisces ♓ and Neptune ♆. Pisces is about the desire to serve others because the personality has been destructive in past lifetimes. To OVERCOME self negativity, pity, doubt and oversensitivity of a psychic or clairvoyant nature, to accommodate the need to reshape the personality with the current zodiac sun sign, to show oneness of life.

The Australian Bush Flower Remedy that helps with these matters is – Fringed Violet and also Sydney Rose.

The issue for this house is learning to develop a spiritual lifestyle of UNIVERSAL UNDERSTANDING.

CHAPTER 3

Well, to jump on the theme of the Matrix movies, the planets of our solar system (and for all I know other things 'out there'), are the main components of the creation matrix of manifestation in our lives.

As you read through this chapter there is an albeit brief explanation of how we are creating our reality (or, when we aren't conscious of it, how it creates us!!!).

Now, since it takes about 26,000 years for the planets to line up the same way twice, we are all "snowflakes" with a unique character, talents and gifts that no other human has. This is why as individuals we are so important to the collective. To give you an example of how this works, just imagine what it would have been like if the BEE GEE's had not contributed their musical gifts to the rest of us? The world would be so much lesser if that hadn't happened, and as a collective we would not have had the choice of enjoying their music.

So it doesn't matter who you are or what your situation is, YOU HAVE A CONTRIBUTION TO MAKE, and it's up to you whether that comes to pass, or you go through your life until its over without doing that.

YOUR CHOICE……..

When we as individuals lose – the whole world does. When we as individuals win the whole world wins.

ASTROLOGY - THE PLANETS AND YOU. A NATURAL PERSPECTIVE TO THE RELATIONSHIP BETWEEN YOU AND THE COSMOS.

Astrology is a concept that there is a synchronistic correlation between the universe and specific activity on earth.

The uses and application of the science of Astrology has changed enormously since ancient times to the present day. In ancient times it was only available to royalty and certainly not to women.

When I first started Astrology it was being used in a third dimensional way to give "readings" on what would happen if you did nothing and remained unconscious.

Then the 90's came and we realised that we create our own realities and we just might have something to do with what happens in our lives.

Now in the 00's we are realising Astrology can be utilised as a tool for personal evolvement, ascension, and to become conscious of things like the life's purpose, identification of the origins of difficulties in the life of a person, and the future influences affecting the life of a person. So you can in fact function in a conscious awareness that allows the fulfillment of our potentials.

So Astrology has now arrived to a point where it is available to the masses on many levels, and also in many applications, and it's time for this ancient wisdom to spread.

Astrology can be used as a tool to look at our lives and answer the questions of: -

1.   Who am I?

2.   Why am I here?

3.   Is there a higher meaning to life?

Spiritual Astrology comes from the premise that there is a divine part of us that is seeking expression, and that the higher purpose of our lives is to connect with that part of us.

Astrology is the oldest form of psychology and is a system of knowledge that can deliver self-understanding and information, so we can consciously enrich our lives in harmony with nature and our fellow man. The horoscope is truly a tool for self-discovery.

I would now like to take you on a journey through the heavenly bodies in our Solar System and examine how their energies can be used for self-empowerment and life management, and how each planet is a layer of our consciousness and the structure of our reality.

I would also like to re-connect you to some of the correspondences these planetary energies have with the mineral kingdom, numerology and the tarot.

So let us look at the central core of our solar system –

THE SUN

"The Sun is matter and the Sun is spirit". H.P.Blavatsky.

The Sun is like the conductor of the orchestra. If any of the players of that orchestra (the planets) play off-key, then we don't sound good or feel good, and they need to be brought back into balance to play harmoniously and in tune.

The Sun relates to the individuality and the things we need in life to be happy. The Sun is what we have come to be – our inner self. The Sun represents the part of you that wants to shine and be radiant with confidence. So on Sundays we remember our spirit by expressing or doing or being ourselves and it is traditionally a day of re-creation and/ or self- expression.

Everything in nature depends on the Sun's shining light and it constitutes the central life principle of all living things.

The Sun is the mechanism of will, and the astrological sign it is placed in describes an important synthetic focal point of the conscious personality. The condition of the Sun in a persons horoscope (whether strongly or weakly placed) tells how the person used their authority in past lives and how that may need re-balancing this lifetime.

This glowing ball of energy also shows the capacity for love – either the love of power - or the power of love as it rules your power urges or the lack of.

As stars go, the Sun may be small, but we couldn't exist without it. The sun is the only real source of light in our Solar System. If you want to find the true source of light in your own life, then focus on the Sun in your own horoscope.

When you unlock the creative potential of your Sun Sign you experience a sense of cohesion and the feeling of "being yourself".

When we say "Many Happy Returns" on birthdays it means the Sun has returned to the position it was at the time of your birth and we hope your life will consist of many happy ones.

The Sun rules the sign of LEO – love through creativity. The spiritual lesson for the sign of LEO is humility and to creatively express love through the heart centre. So if you are a LEO person then the stones of Amber (fossilised sunshine) and Topaz will assist you to harmonise with the Sun's energy.

The number FIVE (5) is associated with the Sun and Leo as well as the Tarot card THE SUN card No. 19.

THE MOON

Just as the moon moves the tides or the oceans twice a day, so do the Moon's energies affect ALL living things. The Moon relates to the emotions, how we express them and what we become emotional about. The Moon denotes where we have been and the instinctual emotional attitudes based on past experiences.

This is the part of you that wants safety and security. In short the Moon is the soul while the Sun is the spirit and the soul is the clothing that the spirit wears.

The Moon rules the sign of CANCER. The spiritual lesson for the sign of Cancer is to let go. So if you are a Cancer person, the Moonstone and the Pearl will assist you to harmonise with the Moon's energy.

The number Two (2) is associated with the Moon and Cancer as well as the Tarot card THE MOON No. 18.

THE PLANET MERCURY

Mercury relates to communication, how we communicate and what we communicate about. It rules the faculties of reason and the intellect. This is the part of you that wants to learn.

Mercury rules the sign of Gemini (and Virgo) and the spiritual lesson for the sign of Gemini is to learn to focus and concentrate. So if you are a Gemini person the two gemstones that will assist you to harmonise with the Mercurial energy are Adventurine and Amozonite.

"As a man thinketh, so he is." Unknown

The number Three (3) is associated with the planet Mercury as is the Magician card No. 1.

THE PLANET VENUS

Venus is the planet of relating and Venus relates to the way we show our love. In a woman's chart how she likes people to see her. In a man's chart it signifies the 'right' type of partner for him. This is the part of you that wants to love and be loved.

The basic personality function of Venus is to develop an awareness of others. The people represented by this planet are women and children.

Venus rules the signs of Libra and Taurus. The spiritual lessons for Libra are co-operation and decisiveness. The stones of Pink Tourmaline and Topaz assist Librans to acquire harmony and balance. The spiritual lesson for Taurus is detachment to people and things so security can come from within. The stones that will assist Taureans are Jade and Carnelian.

The number Four (4) is associated with Taurus as is the Tarot card the Heirophant No. 5.

The number Six (6) is associated with Libra as is the Tarot card Adjustment No. 8.

THE PLANET MARS

Mars relates to the way we use our energy and drive. In a man's chart Mars indicates how he sees himself and in a woman's chart Mars indicates the 'right' type of man for her.

This is the part of you that wants to be independent and assertive and where the energy that motivates our desire nature comes from.

The planet Mars rules the sign of Aries. The Aries spiritual lesson is about patience and the courage to become self- aware. The stones to help Aries people to be in tune with themselves are Garnet and Bloodstone.

The number One (1) is associated with Aries as is the Tarot card the Tower card No. 16.

THE PLANET JUPITER

Jupiter is the planet that relates to self-expansion and personal growth. This self-expansion comes through the use of the sign Jupiter is placed in. This is the part of you that wants social interaction and the opportunity to expand.

The sign that Jupiter rules is Sagittarius – the archer. The spiritual lesson for Sagittarius is restraint – to not be overly indulgent and to be a truth seeker who gathers wisdom.

The stones to harmonise the Sagittarian energy are Tourquoise and Jasper.

The number 22 is associated with Sagittarius as is the Tarot card Fortune card No. 10.

THE PLANET SATURN

Saturn in the horoscope indicates our areas of responsibility, karma, and our fears and phobias. Saturn shows our fears in the area related to the sign it is placed in, and the need to do well, and the fear that you won't.

This is the part of you that wants stability, recognition, rules and yes even limits.

Saturn rules the sign of Capricorn and the spiritual lesson is social-ability.

The stones to harmonise the Capricorn energy are the Sapphire and Onyx.

The number Eight (8) is associated with Capricorn as is the Tarot card The Universe card No. 21.

TO PROGRESS FURTHER IN CONSCIOUSNESS, WE MUST PASS SATURN'S TESTS AND GO BEYOND OUR LIMITATIONS, TO THE TRANSPERSONAL PLANETS INTO INTERGALACTIC CONSCIOUSNESS OF THE LAST FOUR HEAVENLY BODIES OF OUR SOLAR SYSTEM.

THE PLANET(OID) CHIRON

Chiron is the Rainbow Bridge between the inner and outer planets. This planetoid relates to the part of you that wants to heal yourself and others. This energy relates to the wound of the soul. Chiron rules the concept that when you heal yourself you heal the planet.

Chiron rules the sign of Virgo. The spiritual lesson is tolerance – to stop judging themselves and instead understand themselves.

The stones to help attune to this energy are Moss Agate and Rhodoachrosite. Chiron rules crystal healing and you may have noticed how popular crystals became after this planetoid was discovered in 1977.

The number Six (6) is associated with Virgo as is the Tarot card the Hermit No. 9.

THE NEXT THREE PLANETS ARE THE PLANETS OF THE HIGHER OCTAVE – THE TRANSPERSONAL PLANETS.

THE PLANET URANUS.

This planet represents the higher octave of the Mercurial energies. Uranus relates to the energy that clears away old ideas to make us see with a new and clear sight. Its function is to awaken. This is the part of you that wants to take risks and be spontaneous. This is the force for awakening higher consciousness.

The Sign that this planet rules is Aquarius. The spiritual lesson for Aquarius is warmth.

The stones to allow originality and intuition are :- Lapis Lazuli and Howlite.

The corresponding numbers to this energy are 9 and 11.

The Tarot card that resonates with this planet is the Star card no. 17 which is very futuristic, a card of hopes and wishes for humanity and cosmic inspirations.

THE PLANET NEPTUNE

Neptune is the higher octave of Venus. This planet relates to all areas of life without boundaries, like liquids, music, art, colour, dance, mysticism. Neptune also rules areas where things aren't clear and where and you can have illusions. Neptune brings cosmic truths which go far beyond the powers of reason. This is the part of you that wants to dream and fantasise. This is the bestower of universal love.

The sign ruled by this planet is Pisces. The Pisces spiritual lesson is perseverance, and to develop universal understanding so they don't drift.

The stones which will assist Pisces are the Amethyst and Aquamarine.

The number that corresponds to Neptune is 33/6.

The Tarot card that relates to this planet is the Hanged Man No. 12 the card of surrender.

THE PLANET PLUTO

This is the higher octave of Mars. This planet relates to self-transformation and power. Pluto rules the underworld, the dark forces and evolution. We are being taught to see that the light only exists because darkness also exists. We are learning that we will never know our divinity until we also look at our shadow.

This is the part of you that you may not want to know (the shadow).

The sign ruled by Pluto is Scorpio and the Scorpio spiritual lesson is about forgiveness – to let go of control and allow love to flow, trusting that all will be well.

The Stones that will assist this process are Obsidian and Jet.

The number corresponding to Pluto is no. 7.

The Tarot card that aligns with this energy is of course the Death card No.13. Death meaning transformation and change, change being the only constant as everything passes.

So there we have the basic structure of reality.

Mankind has progressed at a furious rate in the last 200 plus years, since the discovery of Uranus in 1781, when the French Revolution soon followed and human rights and equality for all was the cause.

Then in 1846 Neptune was discovered and Spiritualism soon followed.

In 1930 Pluto was discovered, which gave birth to the atomic age, and bought man to the realisation that he could harness the creative and destructive forces embodied in the seed of life, the atom.

The newest member of the Solar System Chiron was discovered in 1977. Chiron is a bridge from the inner planets up to Saturn to the outer planets, which are developing Mankind towards galactic consciousness.

CHAPTER FOUR

Now I have wondered all my life why I was born and what I was doing here. I HAVE NEVER STOPPED WONDERING THAT EITHER!!! That is until I started learning Astrology in my late 30's and I realised that IT WAS POSSIBLE TO KNOW THE ANSWER TO THAT QUESTION.

We are lead to beLIEve that it is not possible to answer this fundamental life question...............after all if we had meaning and purpose in our lives, what a difference it would make to not only our own lives, but also our world. I have concluded that our "systems" of education and socialisation are the main reason for us not finding our direction and purpose, and I have also concluded that this is done on purpose to disempower us and keep us ignorant. After all aren't we so much easier to control in this ignorant and disempowered state.

Okay, so I can understand that you might not want to take my word for that. I challenge you and invite you now to investigate this for yourself – learn to inform yourself of the truth about your own life and life itself!! If what I am saying isn't true then why weren't we taught things like LIFE SKILLS or COPING STRATEGIES in any part of the school life!! That subject that is called Personal Development hasn't spawned any results in my opinion.

So what are you doing here anyway?

What is your life purpose?

Astrology has a wonderful technique that can use the horoscope of an individual to determine the life purpose and lessons that the person has come to learn. This technique is called the Nodes of the Moon, or the NORTH NODE and SOUTH NODE AXIS. This nodal axis is not a planet but a point in space where the moon cuts the ecliptic (the orbit of the Earth around the Sun).

To quote Martin Schulman – "to a qualified expert, a knowledge of the Sun, Moon and Nodal positions can reveal the entire life of the individual"

So how many people know their MOON SIGN??????????

Not many!!! It makes you wonder doesn't it why the Sun Sign information is so readily available, but the Moon Sign, the part of us that is the unconscious, the phobias the habits from past lives and the nature of our emotions and instincts is so unavailable. In fact, a lot of people are even unaware that the Moon or any other planet other than the Sun (the Sun is a Star) has anything to do with them!

So, to cut a long story really short the Sun is what we are learning to become and the Moon rules the past and our emotional natures.

It is as though the Moon, which displays the personality and is the sum total of the past experiences, uses the Nodes to display the future direction of development towards becoming what the Sun is indicating in the chart. What the Sun is indicating by the house placement is covered in the previous chapter, however to know fully what the Sun is indicating you would have to examine the ASPECTS of the Sun in the horoscope.

I have used the Nodes in the chart as an indication of the life purpose, and to define the particular life issues and lessons and the pathway towards future evolution for the person. I would even say that the Nodes of the Moon are a doorway that when opened answers many questions as to how and why we have the lives we have.

No Nodal sign is more desirable than the other and it seems that as in all things a balance is required to integrate both ends into the persons life. When this balance of the Nodal Axis is acquired then the polarity 'lifts off' and ascension happens. Ascension is only the removal of emotional blocks and that is the main reason this information is so valuable to the individual.

I also believe that the knowledge of a persons moon sign is unavailable is because the moon is a persons FEMININE energy and as everyone knows the feminine has been surpressed for thousands of years. So all those "macho" individuals out there can't be a balanced person (and therefore disempowered) because of the denial of the feminine side.

The SOUTH NODE is a pool of knowledge and experiences/ideas/attitudes and thoughts whose unresolved effects are creating the current experiences. The South Node is also a repository of ingrained habits that are a foundation to rest on and a comfort zone, even though they are probably dysfunctional. There is karmic patterns and residue here.

So to balance the Nodal Axis the South Node issues must be resolved and worked through so the North Node GROWTH and EVOLUTION can take place. It's the aspects to this axis that mitigate or hinder this process.

The North Node actually shows us this direction to take to grow towards and when this growth occurrs, personal power and evolutionary growth is achieved.

AT THIS POINT I MUST MAKE IT CLEAR TO YOU AS A HUMAN BEING THE ONLY THING WE HAVE COME TO LIVE FOR IS EVOLUTIONARY GROWTH AND PROGRESS.

EVOLUTIONARY GROWTH AND PROGRESS IS THE ONLY THING WE TAKE WITH US OUT OF THIS LIFE WHEN WE LEAVE IT.

HEARSES DO NOT HAVE TRAILERS!!!!

To quote Martin Schulman again "The Nodes are actually points of soul magnetism one pulling towards the future and one coming from the past".

So next we come to the planetary ruler of the sign (which can be found in Chapter One) of the North Node. This ruling planet of the astrological sign that the Node is in indicates, by its placement and aspects, a further expression to the nodal energies.

Martin Lass who is another wonderful exponent of Spiritual Astrology looks at the nodes in this way –

"The signs will indicate the energetic nature of the path – what lessons and potentials are in a broad sense.

The House placement will give that path a context within real life – it's the stage upon which the souls path is acted out."

.........now I can't improve on that.

There is something that I wish to point out to you before you find out your DIRECTION IN LIFE and what your LIFE PURPOSE is concerned with. Whatever Astrological Sign your North Node is in is where you have had little or no previous experience in, so because of this you WON'T have confidence in these areas, which is exactly why you have chosen this lifetime to work towards it!!! So you will BE AFRAID and you will be INHIBITED and AWKWARD in this area.

So now why don't you have a look at your North Node for yourself. You can look up your Nodal Sign by locating your date of birth on the following table. However the house position must be obtained from your horoscope. Please remember that this is a Nodal AXIS so the South Node will be the sign opposite the North Node. To find the sign opposite the North Node Sign just look at the Sign in the First Chapter.

THE LOCATION OF YOUR NORTH NODE

Locate the span that includes your birth date in the chart below. Your North Node position is listed to the right of these dates.

May 10,1899-Jan 21,1901 Sagittarius
Jan 22,1901-July 21,1902 Scorpio
July 22, 1902-Jan 15,1904 Libra
Jan 16,1904-Sept 18,1905 Virgo
Sept 19,1905-Mar 30,1907 Leo
Mar 31,1907-Sept 27,1908 Cancer
Sept 28,1908-Mar 23,1910 Gemini
Mar 24,1910-Dec 8,1911 Taurus
Dec 9,1911-June 6,1913 Aries
June 7,1913-Dec 3,1914 Pisces
Dec 4,1914-May 31,1916 Aquarius
June 1,1916-Feb 13,1918 Capricorn
Feb 14,1918-Aug 15,1919 Sagittarius
Aug 16,1919-Feb 7,1921 Scorpio
Feb 8, 1921-Aug 23,1922 Libra

Apr 20,1969-Nov 2,1970 Pisces
Nov 3,1970-Apr 27,1972 Aquarius
Apr 28,1972-Oct 27,1973 Capricorn
Oct 28,1973-July 10,1975 Sagittarius
July 11,1975-Jan 7,1977 Scorpio
Jan 8,1977-July 5,1978 Libra
July 6,1978-Jan 12,1980 Virgo
Jan 13,1980-Jan 12,1980 Virgo
Sept 25,1981-Mar 16,1983 Cancer
Mar 17,1983-Sept 11,1984 Gemini
Sept 12,1984-Apr 6,1986 Taurus
Apr 7,1986-Dec 2,1987 Aries
Dec 3,1987-May 22,1989 Pisces
May 23,1989-Nov 18,1990 Aquarius
Nov 19, 1990-Aug 1,1992 Capricorn
Aug 2,1992-Feb 1,1994 Sagittarius
Feb 2,1994-July 31,1995 Scorpio
Aug 1, 1995-Jan 25,1997 Libra
Jan 26,1997-Oct 20,1998 Virgo
Oct 21,1998-Apr 9,2000 Leo

Aug 24,1922-Apr 23,1924 Virgo
Aug 24,1924-Oct 26,1925 Leo
Oct 27,1925-Apr 16,1927 Cancer
Apr 17,1927-Dec 28,1928 Gemini
Dec 29,1928-July 7,1930 Taurus
July 8,1930-Dec 28,1931 Aries
Dec 29,1931-June 24, 1933 Pisces
June 25,1933-Mar 8,1935 Aquarius
Mar 9,1935-Sept 14,1936 Capricorn
Sept 15,1936-Mar 3,1938 Sagittarius
Mar 4,1938-Sept 12,1939 Scorpio
Sept 13,1939- May 24 1941 Libra
May 5,1941-Nov 2,1942 Virgo
Nov 22,1942-May 11,1944 Leo
May 12,1944-Dec 13,1945 Cancer

Apr 10,2000-Oct 12,2001 Cancer
Oct 13,2001-Apr 13,2003 Gemini
Apr 14,2003-Dec 25,2004 Taurus
Dec 26,2004-June 21,2006 Aries
June 22,2006-Dec 18,2007 Pisces
Dec 19,2007-Aug 21,2009 Aquarius
Aug 22,2009-Mar 3,2011 Capricorn
Mar 4,2011-Aug 29,2012 Sagittarius
Aug 30,2012-Feb 18,2014 Scorpio
Feb 19,2014-Nov 11,2015 Libra
Nov 12,2015-May 9,2017 Virgo
May 10,2017-Nov 6,2018 Leo
Nov 7,2018-May 4,2020 Cancer
May 5,2020-Jan 18,2022 Gemini
Jan 19,2022-July 17,2023 Taurus
July 18,2023-Jan 11,2025 Aries
Jan 12,2025-July 26,2026 Pisces
July 17,2026-Mar 26,2028 Aquarius
Mar 27,2028-Sept 23,2029 Capricorn
Sept 24,2029-Mar 20,2031 Sagittarius

Dec 14,1945-Aug 2,1947 Gemini
Aug 3,1947-Jan 26,1949 Taurus
Jan 27,1949-July 26,1950 Aries
July 27,1950-Mar 28,1952 Pisces
Mar 29,1952-Oct 9,1953 Aquarius
Oct 10,1953-Apr 2,1955 Capricorn
Apr 3,1955-Oct 4,1956 Sagittarius
Oct 5,1956-June 16,1958 Scorpio
June 17,1958-Dec 15,1959 Libra
Dec 16,1959-June 10,1961 Virgo
June 11,1961-Dec 23,1962 Leo
Dec 24,1962-Aug 25,1964 Cancer
Aug 26,1964-Feb 19,1966 Gemini
Feb 20,1966-Aug 19,1967 Taurus
Aug 20,1967-Apr 19,1969 Aries

Mar 21,2031-Dec 1,2032 Scorpio
Dec 2,2032-June 3,2034 Libra
June 4,2034-Nov 29,2035 Virgo
Nov 30,2035-May 29,2037 Leo
May 30,2037-Feb 9,2039 Cancer
Feb 10,2039-Aug 10,2040 Gemini
Aug 11,2040-Feb 3,2042 Taurus
Feb 4,2042-Aug 19,2043 Aries
Aug 19,2043-Apr 18,2045 Pisces
Apr 19,2045-Oct 18,2046 Aquarius
Oct 19,2046-Apr 11,2048 Capricorn
Apr 12,2048-Dec 14,2049 Sagittarius
Dec 15,2049-June 28,2051 Scorpio

THE ARIES NORTH NODE OR THE NORTH NODE IN THE FIRST HOUSE

• There is a need to BECOME INDEPENDENT.

• Aries means new growth – A new approach to life is needed and living it through your own efforts.

• Learning "to stand on your own two feet" not depending on others.

• Getting the BALANCE of self Vs other(s). This is the Relationship polarity – if you don't have yourself then you don't relate well to others.

• Courage and bravery. Having the courage to become self-aware. It takes more courage to look at yourself than if does to look at others.

• Self-sufficiency Vs Dependency.

• Without this SELF- DEVELOPMENT you run the risk of dysfunctional relationships.

AFFIRMATION: "WHEN I DO WHAT IS RIGHT FOR MYSELF, I DO WHAT IS RIGHT FOR EVERYONE."

ANTIDOTES FOR BALANCING ARIES NORTH NODE OR NORTH NODE IN THE FIRST HOUSE:

• Take a risk (not a dangerous one!).

• Self-assertiveness training.

• Any sort of self-discipline programme could prove beneficial.

• Try something new – anything that will promote the growth of the personality.

• Wearing the colour bright red would be inspirational and envigorating.

• Take a journey of SELF- DISCOVERY.

• Take the Australian Bush Flower Essences of Red Grevillea, Macrocarpa, Mountain Devil and Black-Eyed Susan.

THE UNDERLYING LESSON IS ONE OF PATIENCE..........

THE TAURUS NORTH NODE OR NORTH NODE IN THE SECOND HOUSE

• Learning that security comes from within and not from external things and other people.

•These people need to DEVELOP their personal resources and talents and value them appropriately.

•Sexual issues – Lower desires Vs higher motive. There could be a preoccupation with sex or addiction. This is typical of power sourced externally.

•To become more sensual and to enjoy the senses.

•To develop a set of personal values to live by. This value system may need re-adjustment from past lives to new and more unconditional/ spiritual ones so that loyalty/honesty and integrity prevail.

•To develop a nurturing connection to Mother Earth and become more practical. This is also important to ground the person to the here and now.

•There is a tendency here to be a 'victim' of others from past lives as indicated by the negative endings of the house position.

•To make sure that you own your possessions and that they don't own you.

AFFIRMATION: "WHEN I LIVE BY MY OWN VALUES, I FEEL GOOD ABOUT MYSELF."

ANTIDOTES FOR TAURUS NORTH NODE OR NORTH NODE IN THE SECOND HOUSE.

•Gardening (even if it is in pots). This connects these people with the earth, making them more practical and soothed by nature, slowing them down to clear the head.

•Creating something from yourself that gives you self-worth also attunes to the Taurean energy.

•Using any known 'grounding' technique. For example walking on the beach with bare feet is good.

•Learning how to create abundance through keeping a gratitude journal. The practice of writing how you are grateful for five things each day can change your whole value system.

•Wearing the colour pink is good to stimulate the Taurean energy.

•Take the Australian Bush Flowers of Bauhinia, Old Man Banksia, Five Corners and Wisteria.

•THE UNDERLYING LESSON IS ONE OF DETATCHMENT.

THE GEMINI NORTH NODE OR NORTH NODE IN THE THIRD HOUSE

•These people are learning to communicate.

•These people are also being invited to actively participate in the community, and in doing so must communicate!

•These people must work towards using their intellectual abilities and their mental talents.

•They need to learn to 'know' through knowledge and to learn from people in their environment (neighbours, relatives, siblings etc.).

•There is sometimes from past lives religious karma here where the person may have been embroiled in a belief System that did not allow free thought and therefore imprisoning their consciousness.

•These people need to educate themselves and may well be repelled by reading or education, although not lacking in intelligence. Often there are learning difficulties because of being unable to stay in the 'now' or the moment.

AFFIRMATION: "WHEN I TUNE IN TO HOW OTHERS THINK, I KNOW WHAT TO SAY".

ANTIDOTES FOR BALANCING THE GEMINI NORTH NODE OR NORTH NODE IN THE THIRD HOUSE

•Learning anything at all, and to do this they must listen.

•Learning a language.

•Writing fiction or correspondence encourages interaction of thought.

•Teaching anything at all as a practical way to put knowledge and learning to use.

•The colour to wear or visualise (mental sign) is purple to attune to the Gemini energy.

•Take the Australian Bush Flower Essences of Jacaranda, Bush Fuchsia, Isopogon and Boronia.

THE UNDERLYING LESSON IS ONE OF MENTAL FOCUS.

CANCER NORTH NODE OR NORTH NODE IN THE FOURTH HOUSE

•Learning to nurture. Becoming a more nurturing person to yourself and therefore others. There are many people who do not know how to look after themselves and have no idea what things are not good for them.

•These people are learning through emotional experiences how to feel. These emotional experiences are to facilitate the breaking up of old emotional patterns.

•The domestic relationships (home and family) are an issue for spiritual growth.

•There is a need for public recognition, which opposes domestic responsibilities.

•With this nodal placement there is sometimes a problem with a parent, or the person is learning to become a nurturing, caring parent.

•Learning to be more receptive to feelings and being more sensitive to allow the intuition to become stronger, so that the feminine energy is returned to balance.

•Noticing and validating feelings.

AFFIRMATION: "I LET GO AND FLOW WITH MY FEELINGS."

ANTIDOTES TO CANCER NORTH NODE OR NORTH NODE IN THE FOURTH HOUSE.

•Housekeeping can be good to steer the person back to their "home base" and personal nurturance.

•Researching the family tree can give an awareness of their roots and family patterns.

•Careers in a nurturing profession, such as nursing, catering, hospitality or childcare would all lead to tapping into the Cancer energy.

•Have a dinner party where the nurturing of close friends and family in the home encourages caring communication.

•Go to a health retreat and pamper yourself then take what you learn home and do it there.

•Colours that stimulate the Cancer North Node are smokey colours especially grey.

•Take the Australian Bush Flower Essences of Bottlebrush, She Oak, Alpine Mint Bush and Flannel Flower.

THE UNDERLYING LESSON IS ONE OF LETTING-GO.

THE LEO NORTH NODE OR THE NORTH NODE IN THE FIFTH HOUSE

•Leo rules the HEART so this is about learning to get to the heart of the matter! Also learning to listen to your hearts desire. The person is coming from a long habitual pattern of avoiding matters of the heart.

•Learning to love and open up the heart centre so that loving on a one-to-one basis is possible. Also learning HOW to love.

•There may be eccentric habit patterns to overcome.

•Learning to become more self-expressive and becoming more creative.

•To reveal your creativity/dramatic talents by expressing from an open and flowing heart chakra.

•Centering oneself in personal power. Becoming a leader that serves with power from the heart and gives out love and creativity in the act of expression of the true self.

•Developing the will and inner strength.

AFFIRMATION; "WHEN I BRING JOY TO OTHERS I FEEL INCLUDED."

ANTIDOTES FOR THE LEO NORTH NODE OR NORTH NODE IN THE FIFTH HOUSE

•Risk doing something you haven't done before.

•Take up some sort of creative pursuit.

•Take time out to participate in a recreational activity or sport.

•Get involved with anything to do with the theatre – even if it is behind the scenes.

•Dress yourself in a more self-expressive way, wearing the colours of gold or yellow or cream.

•Take the Australian Bush Flower Essences of Bluebell, Turkey Bush,

Gymea Lily,Waratah and Sturt Desert Rose.

•Looking at yourself in the mirror and saying "I love myself".

THE UNDERLYING LESSON IS ONE OF WARMTH.

VIRGO NORTH NODE OR THE NORTH NODE IN THE SIXTH HOUSE

- Virgo is about bringing your dreams down to earth.

- Becoming more grounded, systematic and more practical.

- Being of service to others without self- interest.

- These people need to develop discrimination as to whether something is viable or not.

- Developing a care for details.

- Focusing on the here and now using the conscious mind to actually keep yourself in the now moment.

- Bringing order and a system to their somewhat chaotic lifestyle. There is a need to stop drifting aimlessly and spending large amounts of time in 'no-where land' or 'off-with-the-fairies'.

- Taking personal responsibility for the state of their own health and realising that self- healing is possible.

- Learning about healing yourself and others (this is to do with the Planet Chiron).

AFFIRMATION: "WHEN I FOCUS AND HAVE A PLAN THE WHOLE UNIVERSE OPENS THE PATHWAY TO SUCCESS."

ANTIDOTES FOR THE VIRGO NORTH NODE OR NORTH NODE IN THE SIXTH HOUSE

- Gardening to ground the person into the here and now and to promote a more systematic way of thinking – clarity.

- Typing and computer work – more system and order.

- Music and/or playing a musical instrument.

- Any kind of volunteer work.

- Making lists or scheduling activities with chores to get a balanced routine going, whilst still remaining flexible.

•The colour to wear or to visualise to stimulate the Virgo energy would be light blue.

•Take the Australian Bush Flower Essences of Sundew, Red Lily, Spinifex and Fringed Violet.

THE UNDERLYING LESSON IS ONE OF ACCEPTANCE AND TOLERANCE.

THE NORTH NODE IN LIBRA OR THE NORTH NODE IN THE SEVENTH HOUSE

•This nodal placement is not only about learning to relate to others period, its also about learning to relate to others in harmony and co-operation.

•To relate to others harmoniously then you must have INNER PEACE. Without inner peace (say you have hostility, frustration and anger instead) it isn't possible to relate harmoniously because the discomfort of inner turmoil doesn't allow the person to be aware of the other.

•These people are learning to develop an appreciation for the arts.

•Libra is about learning to share and co-operate in the dance of life. There may be a tendency to want to be alone, or choose solitude because of lack of confidence relating to others.

•Self-interest, or a self-orientation, needs to be balanced with consideration of the needs of others, becoming more aware of how the stimuli provided by ourselves is the cause of others reactions and responses.

•The more one fights the more one loses – aggression must be tempered with peace.

•The Libra North Node is learning about creating Win/Win situations.

AFFIRMATION: "WHEN I SHARE WITH OTHERS I HAVE MORE".

ANTIDOTES TO BALANCE THE LIBRA NORTH NODE OR NORTH NODE IN THE SEVENTH HOUSE.

•Activities should be sought out that require partnership and teamwork.

•Any kind of support position, where their strong sense of identity can be used.

•Play tennis – mixed doubles.

•Getting involved in anything to do with the arts. The art of beauty, design, fashion, even architecture or anything to do with creating harmony.

•The colours to stimulate the Libra Node are all the pastel shades. You may wear them or visualise them.

•Take the Australian Bush Flower Essences of Mulla Mulla, Dog Rose, Tall Mulla Mulla, Tall Yellow Top and Bush Gardenia.

THE UNDERLYING LESSON IS ONE OF CO-OPERATION.

THE NORTH NODE OF SCORPIO OR THE NORTH NODE IN THE EIGHTH HOUSE.

•These people are learning to regenerate themselves through the transformational process of FORGIVENESS.

•The passive resistance to CHANGE in their lives causes stagnation and therefore robs these people of their regenerative abilities. They are learning that to change is to grow and the only alternative to change is stagnation. When stagnation occurrs the persons internal energy systems get blocked – not good.

•Self-worth and/or a high degree of self esteem is necessary – no self-worth = no Power! So if the self-worth is low it must be healed to allow the Value Axis to be balanced.

•These people are learning that to CHANGE IS TO GROW.

•There is a tendency to plod through life or to be encased in a large comfort zone or 'rut'. The biggest growth occurs when they are able to 'let go' of materialistic desires.

•The main issue of this nodal placement is POWER and its harmonious utilisation. Power when wielded is very negative and destructive and this must be understood. Authentic power is from within. Power sourced externally is addiction.

AFFIRMATION: "CHANGE IS THE ONLY CONSTANT, NOT TO CHANGE IS IMPOSSIBLE."

ANTIDOTES FOR THE SCORPIO NORTH NODE OR THE NORTH NODE IN THE EIGHTH HOUSE.

•Study the ancient mysteries to uncover the secrets to life.

•Explore the birth/death and rebirth cycle so an understanding is reached of the transformational process of life.

•Become a member of a meditation group where self-analysis is supported and personal change is fostered.

•The colour to stimulate the Scorpio energy is Maroon.

•Take the Australian Bush Flower Essences of Bush Iris, Billy Goat

Plum, Daggar Hakea and Mint Bush.

THE UNDERLYING LESSON IS ONE OF SELF-EMPOWERMENT.

NORTH NODE IN SAGITTARIUS OR THE NORTH NODE IN THE NINTH HOUSE

•These people are learning to become truth seekers. They must seek to live their own truth and also learn the truth about life.

•They must learn the 'Higher' meanings to life.

•This nodal placement is about learning to become more philosophical and less engaged in trivial, time wasting activities where scattered thinking doesn't allow insight.

•This Node is learning to develop a sense of freedom and adventure. These people need to pursue 'other' philosophies and different cultures to attain wisdom. Getting embroiled in meaningless activities that don't allow focused thought will prevent this.

•Studying in order to develop mentally and spiritually so higher wisdom is attained. They must aspire towards balancing the left brain with the right so that the balance allows 'higher" thinking so 'bigger' possibilities are contemplated.

•They are learning to perceive and understand the bigger picture of life. To do this they must work towards engaging the Higher Mind on a daily basis. The lower or mundane mind must be brought into balance so it doesn't predominate.

AFFIRMATION: "WHEN I TRUST MY INTUITION AND VERBALLY COMMUNICATE WHAT OCCURS TO ME IN THE MOMENT, I WIN."

ANTIDOTES FOR THE SAGITTARIUS NORTH NODE OR THE NORTH NODE IN THE NINTH HOUSE.

•Join a group travelling to visit another culture and/or religion where there can be a cultural exchange.

•Work as a travel agent or tour guide.

•If you can afford it, go horse riding for that feeling of freedom and wide open spaces.

•Study or learn philosophy – read some of the famous philosophers e.g. Plato.

•The colour to stimulate the Sagittarius energy is Turquoise. You can either wear it or visualise it.

•Take the Australian Bush Flower Essences of Angelsword, Freshwater Mangrove, Sunshine Wattle or Silver Princess.

THE UNDERLYING LESSON IS ONE OF RESTRAINT.

THE NORTH NODE IN CAPRICORN OR THE NORTH NODE IN THE TENTH HOUSE.

•These people are learning personal responsibility. Not responsibility as in burden or obligation, but learning the ABILITY to RESPOND to their life. By taking personal responsibility for creating their own reality they take their power back.

•They are also learning to leave home and take care of themselves. To grow up and mature.

•So this Node is about learning to face up to life as a mature adult and work in the public somehow in a responsible position.

•If these people don't have emotional security then they won't be able to attain outer worldly success, or at least sustain it for long. There is usually a need to overcome emotional family patterns from the past.

•Usually the career will oppose family and vice versa. So its learning to stay goal oriented and not using family problems as an excuse not to circulate in the outside world – particularly in the business world.

AFFIRMATION: "I CANNOT CONTROL OTHERS, BUT I CAN CONTROL MYSELF."

ANTIDOTES FOR CAPRICORN NORTH NODE OR NORTH NODE IN THE TENTH HOUSE.

•Go out – anywhere. These people tend to 'cling' on to others "needing" them so they don't have to achieve anything.

•Leadership roles help these people – like chairperson/president etc.

•Work on an organised plan to achieve a personal ambition of some sort. Make sure there is a rough time-line so boundaries or time limits push the person to not cop-out.

•The colour that stimulates the Capricorn energy is Indigo. You may wear it or visualise it.

•Take the Australian Bush Flower Essences of Southern Cross, Boab, Illawarra Flame Tree, Bottlebrush and Red Helmet Orchid.

THE UNDERLYING LESSON IS ONE OF 'SOCIAL –ABILITY'.

NORTH NODE IN AQUARIUS OR NORTH NODE IN THE ELEVENTH HOUSE

•This nodal placement is learning to become the detached humanitarian.

•There will be opportunities to utilise the original creativity for the good of the collective.

•These people are learning that one-to-one personal love has to progress to humanitarian love for all. This is an impersonal love that is being learned.

•The ego has to be overcome to allow things like – all people are equal, our soul light has no colour, all people have equal human rights, and we are all one, to be learned.

•There is also a lesson to 'ELEVATE' the consciousness to a place where the concept of universal brotherhood is integrated into the life of the person and they exemplify it.

•These people are also learning about friendship and how to have friends, you have to be one to others.

AFFIRMATION:"WHEN I LOVE MYSELF, I LOVE THE WHOLE WORLD."

ANTIDOTES FOR AQUARIUS NORTH NODE OR NORTH NODE IN THE ELEVENTH HOUSE.

•Join a group or organisation that works for the collective good.

•Make an effort to not indulge in personal interests to the extent that you do not develop friendships or participate in social groups

•Be an activist for social change for the highest good of the collective in any way you feel impressed. E.g. world peace.

•Writing about anything to do with humanitarian causes or world problems stimulates yourself and others to inform themselves about what is REALLY going on in this world.

•Inform yourself from independent, credible sources about health issues, world events, spirituality and look at a wide variety of opinions about these things. To inform yourself about the truth you will have to go outside "official sources".

• Use your personal creativity and original ideas in a way that makes a contribution to the whole, don't just keep them to yourself. Become more culturally creative and make other friends that do likewise.

•The colour to wear and visualise to stimulate the Aquarian energy is bright blue.

•Take the Australian Bush Flower Essences of Slender Rice Flower, Gymea Lily, Tall Mulla Mulla and Hibbertia.

THE UNDERLYING LESSON IS ONE OF HUMILITY.

THE PISCES NORTH NODE OR NORTH NODE IN THE TWELFTH HOUSE

•This node is about attaining enlightenment (dropping the fear based mentality) and coming to a point of universal understanding.

•Here the person is developing faith (faith in themselves and their own abilities) instead of reacting to everything with doubt and analysis.

•These people are learning to trust the intuition (right brain) and developing it to be in balance with the left brain.

•They are also learning to transcend judgement and develop compassion.

•So this nodal placement is about developing a universal consciousness where it is understood that all is one and one is all. These people make the most progress by getting to know the spiritual way of life and freeing the mind through meditation and self-reflection, trusting the process of life to bring you your highest good.

AFFIRMATION: "DIVINE RIGHT ACTION IS ALWAYS TAKING PLACE IN MY LIFE. ONLY GOOD COMES FROM EACH EXPERIENCE."

ANTIDOTES FOR THE PISCES NORTH NODE OR NORTH NODE IN THE TWELFTH HOUSE.

•MEDITATION – MEDITATION – MEDITATION.

•Fishing/boating/swimming/bathing.

•Poetry/fairy tales/myths/legends that stimulate your imagination of yourself.

•Relaxation techniques like soft music, aromatherapy, colour visualisation.

•Spiritual instruction and education.

•The colours to stimulate the Pisces energy are violet red, sea green and ocean blue.

•Take the Australian Bush Flower Essences of Fringed Violet, Red

Lily, Yellow Cowslip Orchid and Sydney Rose.

THE UNDERLYING LESSON IS ONE OF SELF-ACCEPTANCE (HEALING).

CHAPTER FIVE

ASTROLOGY AND BUSH FLOWER HEALING

YOU MAY BE WONDERING HOW ASTROLOGY CAN BE "HEALING". YOU MAY ALSO THINK THAT ASTROLOGY IS USED TO TELL THE FUTURE AND I WOULD SAY THAT CAN BE A MISUSE OF THE SCIENCE OF ASTROLOGY (THAT IS ONLY MY OPINION), ALTHOUGH MANY DO THAT. I WOULD PREFER TO SAY THAT ASTROLOGY CAN INDICATE FOR YOU WHAT INFLUENCES WILL BE COMING UP FOR YOU AND HOW TO MAKE THE BEST OF THOSE PARTCIULAR INFLUENCES IN YOUR LIFE .

I AM A SPIRITUAL ASTROLOGER AND I SPECIALISE IN USING THE HOROSCOPE AS A DIAGNOSTIC TOOL FOR PERSONAL DEVELOPMENT, EMPOWERMENT AND ASCENSION.

ASTROLOGY IS A SYSTEM OF ANALYSIS THAT CAN BE USED TO IDENTIFY THE ORIGINS OF BEHAVIOURAL AND PHYSICAL PROBLEMS AND HOW THEY CAN BE RESOLVED AND HEALED. THE HEALING CAN BE MENTAL OR ATTITUDINAL, OR SPIRITUAL IN THAT IT RECONNECTS THE PERSON TO THEIR PATH, AND EMOTIONAL IN THAT YOU CAN MAINTAIN EMOTIONAL BALANCE, AND PHYSICAL AS THIS PROCESS REMOVES ENERGY BLOCKS FROM THE BODY.

THE HOROSCOPE CAN REVEAL SUBCONSCIOUS THINKING AND ATTITUDES THAT SABOTAGE THE PERSON, WHEN THEY MAY HAVE HAD NO CONSCIOUS AWARENESS OF IT PREVIOUSLY.

SO USING THE ASTROLOGICAL HOROSCOPE TO PRESCRIBE THE AUSTRALIAN BUSH FLOWER ESSENCES IS A WONDERFUL COMBINATION TO ASSIST SOMEONE WITH THE INTENTION OF SELF- DEVELOPMENT AND OF COURSE SELF- HEALING.

THERE ARE 66 AUSTRALIAN BUSH FLOWER ESSENCES ALTOGETHER. AS WELL AS COMBINATION MIXES FOR SPECIFIC PURPOSES, E.G. MEDITATION ESSENCE.

I HAVE ALIGNED EACH FLOWER WITH AN ASTROLOGY SIGN AND PLANET. EVERY ASTROLOGY SIGN RULES CERTAIN PARTS OF THE HUMAN BODY, SO THE FLOWERS ALL FIT COMFORTABLY WITHIN THAT FRAMEWORK.

HOWEVER THE BUSH FLOWER ESSENCES CAN BE PRESCRIBED FOR A PHYSICAL PROBLEM OR CONDITION, OR A PARTICULAR REASON LIKE MORE ENERGY, MORE CONFIDENCE, HORMONE BALANCE, OR A CERTAIN ASTROLOGY SIGN, OR EVEN A PARTICULAR BIRTHFORCE NUMBER OR PERSONAL YEAR IN NUMEROLOGY.

THE FUNDAMENTAL CONCEPTS THAT WE CREATE OUR OWN REALITIES AND THAT THE BODY IS AN INDICATOR OF THE SOUL'S BALANCE, IS WHY THIS COMBINATION OF ASTROLOGY AND THE AUSTRALIAN BUSH FLOWER ESSENCES WORK SO WELL.

NOW I WOULD LIKE TO TALK ABOUT A FEW OF THE FLOWERS THEMSELVES SO YOU CAN GET AN IDEA OF THE SORTS OF THINGS THEY DO.

I WILL ONLY COVER THREE OF THEM AND THE THREE I HAVE CHOSEN ARE VERY MUCH FOR WHAT BLOCKS US FROM PROGRESSING.

I SAY "DON'T JUST GO THROUGH LIFE … GROW THROUGH LIFE."

THE FIRST ONE IS -

BOAB

THIS FLOWER IS KEY TO ASCENSION AND SOUL PROGRESS.

HERE IS A QUOTE FROM IAN WHITE'S BOOK "BUSH FLOWER HEALING", WHICH I RECOMMEND THAT YOU READ.

"THE MAIN HEALING QUALITY OF BOAB IS TO CLEAR THE NEGATIVE PATTERNS OF THE ANCESTORS – THE LIMITING DYSFUNCTIONAL, EMOTIONAL AND MENTAL BELIEFS AND PATTERNS THAT ARE INVARIABLY LEARNED AND PASSED

ON FROM GENERATION TO GENERATION. BOAB CAN ACCESS AND CLEAR THESE CORE PATTERNS AND ALL THE RELATED ENSUING BELIEFS."

THE HEALING QUALITIES OF BOAB ARE THAT IT ENGENDERS POSITIVE PERSONAL GROWTH AND ALSO RELEASES NEGATIVE FAMILY BEHAVIOUR AND THOUGHT PATTERNS THAT ARE PASSED DOWN FROM GENERATION TO GENERATION. BOAB HEALS THE EFFECTS OF PREJUDICE, ABUSE AND ANY LIMITING BELIEFS.

IAN WHITE WAS GUIDED TO COLLECT THE FLOWERS FOR THIS REMEDY FROM THE PRISON TREE AT DARBY W.A. LATER THAT NIGHT IN MEDITATION HE ASKED WHY WAS IT THAT HE HAD TO MAKE THE ESSENCE FROM THE PRISON TREE.

THE MESSAGE CAME BACK THAT HUMAN CONSCIOUSNESS HAS BEEN IN CHAINS FOR THOUSANDS OF YEARS AND THAT THIS IS THE ESSENCE TO BREAK THESE CHAINS.

THERE HAS BEEN SOME CHANNELLED INFORMATION INDICATING THAT THE BOAB TREE WAS NOT ORIGINALLY OF EARTH, BUT WAS GIVEN AS A GIFT FROM THE STAR SYSTEM THE PLEIADES. THE BOAB ESSENCE CAN CLEAR 'MIASMS' WHICH ARE PASSED DOWN THROUGH GENERATIONS.

ANGELSWORD

THIS FLOWER COMES FROM THE SNOWY MOUNTAINS.

I'LL QUOTE THE BOOK "BUSH FLOWER HEALING" BY IAN WHITE AGAIN.

"THIS ESSENCE BRINGS OUT AND ENHANCES THE QUALITY OF DISCERNMENT, ALLOWING A PERSON TO CUT THROUGH WITH THE SPIRITUAL SWORD OF DISCERNMENT TO FIND WHAT IS THEIR OWN SPIRITUAL TRUTH.

AT THIS POINT IN TIME MANY PEOPLE ARE GIVING THEIR POWER AWAY BY ACCEPTING THE VALIDITY OF SPIRITUAL MESSAGES, TEACHINGS OR BOOKS WITHOUT QUESTIONING, ESPECIALLY IF THEIR SOURCE IS SEEN TO BE CHANNELLED

FROM A BEING NOT ON THE EARTH PLANE."

ANGELSWORD ALSO ALLOWS YOU TO HEAR THE WORDS OF YOUR OWN ANGEL- YOUR HIGHER SELF AND INNER GUIDANCE. THIS ESSENCE WILL ALSO CLEAR AWAY ANY ATTACHMENTS OR CONFUSION AND ANY NEGATIVE ENTITIES.

SOUTHERN CROSS

THE SOUTHERN CROSS FLOWER WAS COLLECTED FROM THE STIRLING RANGES IN WESTERN AUSTRALIA.

"YOU ARE GIVEN THE GIFTS OF THE GODS.

YOU CREATE YOUR REALITY ACCORDING TO YOUR BELIEFS. YOURS IS THE CREATIVE ENERGY THAT MAKES YOUR WORLD. THERE ARE NO LIMITATIONS TO THE SELF EXCEPT THOSE YOU BELIEVE IN."

JANE ROBERTS

THE SOUTHERN CROSS REMEDY HELPS TO OPEN PEOPLE UP TO THE KNOWLEDGE THAT THIS CAN BE AN ABUNDANT LIFE WITH LOVE AND JOY.

SOUTHERN CROSS IS FOR THE HEALING OF VICTIM AND POVERTY CONSCIOUSNESS TO TAKE A PERSON ONTO PERSONAL POWER/POSITIVITY AND TAKING RESPONSIBILITY.

TO BE ABLE TO RESPOND TO LIFE AS OPPOSED TO REACTING TO IT.

PERSONAL RESPONSIBILITY IS THE MAIN THING THAT OPENS THE HIGH-HEART CHAKRA NEAR THE THYMUS GLAND. THE FLOWER SOUTHERN CROSS IS A POWERFUL FACILITATOR TO THAT PROCESS. WHEN YOU REALISE YOU CREATE THINGS IN YOUR LIFE – YOU REALISE YOU HAVE THE POWER TO CHANGE THEM FOR THE BETTER.

PERSONAL RESPONSIBILITY = PERSONAL POWER.

SOUTHERN CROSS IS ONE OF THE FLOWERS THAT MAKES UP THE CHAKRA BALANCING MIX, WHICH HELPS TO BALANCE EVERY CHAKRA IN THE BODY.

THE FORMULA IS: –

ROOT CHAKRA- BOAB

SACRAL – BOTTLEBRUSH

SOLAR PLEXUS – PEACH FLOWER TEA TREE

HEART – BLUEBELL

HIGH HEART – SOUTHERN CROSS, ILLAWARRA FLAME TREE

THROAT – OLD MAN BANKSIA

THIRD EYE – YELLOW COWSLIP ORCHID

CROWN CHAKRA - ANGELSWORD

I CAN RECOMMEND THIS MIX TO ANYONE WHO DESIRES TO OPERATE AT OPTIMUM LEVELS AND WHO WANTS TO GET MORE OUT OF LIFE, OR AS A STEPPING STONE TO THE WHITE LIGHT ESSENCE RANGE.

THE WHITE LIGHT ESSENCE RANGE ARE 7 VIBRATIONAL ESSENCES COLLECTED FROM SACRED SITES AROUND THE WORLD. THEY ARE THE ELEMENTS, WATER, EARTH, FIRE, AIR, DEVIC, HIGHER- SELF AND ANGELIC ESSENCE.

WATER ESSENCE

WATER ESSENCE WAS COLLECTED FROM THE ISLAND OF IONA IN SCOTLAND IN THE NORTHERN HEMISPHERE AND HERON ISLAND IN THE SOUTHERN HEMISPHERE. THIS ESSENCE IS FOR BALANCING THE EMOTIONS.

EARTH ESSENCE

EARTH ESSENCE WAS COLLECTED FROM A CAVE IN NORTHERN INDIA. THIS ESSENCE IS FOR CLEARING AWAY KARMA AND RECONSTRUCTING YOUR ORIGINAL 12

STRANDS OF DNA.

FIRE ESSENCE

FIRE ESSENCE WAS COLLECTED AT KATAJUTA CENTRAL AUSTRALIA. THE FIRE ESSENCE RECONNECTS YOU TO YOUR "FIERY" SENSE OF PURPOSE AND LIFE DIRECTION AND YOUR SPIRIT.

AIR ESSENCE

AIR ESSENCE WAS COLLECTED ON TOP OF SCHAFBERG MOUNTAIN NEAR ST WOLFGANG AUSTRIA. THE AIR ESSENCE HAS THE QUALITY OF ALLOWING A PERSON TO JOURNEY OUT TO MUCH FURTHER REALMS AND LEVELS ON THE SPIRITUAL PLANE. AIR ESSENCE BALANCES BETWEEN INTELLECTUALISM AND EMOTIONALISM WHILST AIDING DISCRIMINATION AND DISCERNMENT.

HIGHER-SELF ESSENCE.

HIGHER-SELF ESSENCE WAS MADE AT PALENQUE MEXICO. THIS ESSENCE IS FOR A STRONGER CONNECTION TO YOUR HIGHER- SELF.

DEVIC ESSENCE

DEVIC ESSENCE WAS COLLECTED FROM THE CHALICE WELL, AT THE CHALICE WELL GARDENS, GLASTONBURY, ENGLAND.

THIS REMEDY ATTUNES YOU TO NATURE AND THE NATURE OF OURSELVES.

THE ANGELIC ESSENCE

THE ANGELIC ESSENCE WAS COLLECTED FROM THE TOP OF MT PUTUCUSI OVERLOOKING MACHU PICCHU.

THIS ESSENCE HELPS US TO BE MORE OPEN TO RECEIVING FROM THE HIGHER ANGELIC TONES OF INSPIRATION, LOVE, AWARENESS, COMMUNICATION, GUIDANCE AND INSTRUCTION, WHICH CAN LEAD US TO AN INFINITE RANGE

OF POTENTIAL POSSIBILITIES IN OUR MORTAL LIVES.

BELOW IS A "LIST" OF THE AUSTRALIAN BUSH FLOWER ESSENCES AND THEIR ASTROLOGICAL CORRELATIONS.

YOU CAN USE THIS LIST BY LOOKING UP YOUR NODAL AXIS OR YOUR NORTH NODE IN CHAPTER FOUR AND THEN FINDING OUT THE POLARITY YOU ARE ON AND THEN TAKE THE ESSENCES THAT ARE FOR THOSE SIGNS.

EG: IF YOUR NORTH NODE IS THE SIGN OF SCORPIO THEN THE SOUTH NODE WILL BE THE OPPOSITE SIGN OF TAURUS. SO YOUR NODAL AXIS THE "VALUE AXIS" IS WHAT YOU WILL BE WORKING ON. TAKING THE SCORPIO AND TAURUS FLOWERS TO HELP YOU DEVELOP INNER SELF-WORTH YOU WILL AUTHENTICALLY EMPOWER YOURSELF.

ANOTHER EXAMPLE WOULD BE IF YOUR NORTH NODE IS IN THE FOURTH HOUSE (THE HOUSE RULED BY THE SIGN OF CANCER AND THE MOON) AND THE OPPOSITE HOUSE IS THE TENTH HOUSE (THE HOUSE RULED BY CAPRICORN AND SATURN). THESE HOUSES ARE ON THE "SECURITY AXIS" SO YOU WOULD TAKE THE FLOWERS FOR THE SIGNS OF CANCER AND CAPRICORN TO HELP YOU DEVELOP EMOTIONAL SECURITY SO YOU CAN THEN OPERATE WITH CONFIDENCE IN THE OUTSIDE WORLD. EASY!

SO HERE IS THE LIST OF 66 FLOWERS AND THE ASTROLOGICAL SUN SIGN THAT THEY ALIGN WITH.

ARIES.

MOUNTAIN DEVIL
BLACK-EYED SUSAN
KANGAROO PAW
MACROCARPA
RED HELMET ORCHID
MONGA WARATAH

TAURUS

BAUHINIA

FIVE CORNERS
OLD MAN BANKSIA
WILD POTATO BUSH
WISTERIA
CHRISTMAS BELL
PINK FLANNEL FLOWER

GEMINI

BORONIA
BUSH FUCHSIA
ISOPOGON
JACARANDA

CANCER

BOTTLEBRUSH
FLANNEL FLOWER
SHE OAK
STURT DESERT PEA
ALPINE MINT BUSH
RED SUVA FRANGIPANI

LEO

BLUEBELL
STURT DESERT ROSE
TURKEY BUSH
WARATAH
GYMEA LILY
MULLA MULLA

VIRGO

BANKSIA ROBUR
CROWEA
PHILOTHECA
SPINIFEX
YELLOW COWSLIP ORCHID

LIBRA

BUSH GARDENIA
DOG ROSE
PAW PAW
RED GREVILLEA
ROUGH BLUEBELL

SCORPIO

BILLY GOAT PLUM
BUSH IRIS
DAGGER HAKEA
SOUTHERN CROSS
MINT BUSH

SAGITTARIUS

ANGELSWORD
PEACH FLOWER TEA TREE
SILVER PRINCESS
WEDDING BUSH
GREEN SPIDER ORCHID
FRESHWATER MANGROVE

CAPRICORN

HIBBERTIA
ILLAWARRA FLAME TREE
LITTLE FLANNEL FLOWER
BOAB
DOG ROSE OF THE WILD FORCES

AQUARIUS

SLENDER RICE FLOWER
TALL YELLOW TOP
PINK MULLA MULLA
TALL MULLA MULLA

PISCES

FRINGED VIOLET
GREY SPIDER FLOWER

SUNDEW
KAPOK BUSH
RED LILY
SYDNEY ROSE
LICHEN

*PLEASE NOTE THAT THE WHITE LIGHT SPIRITUAL ESSENCES ARE INCORPORATED IN THE SELF-EMPOWERMENT SESSIONS IN PART 2.

<u>HOW TO USE PART 2</u>

Each session starts with either an inspirational verse that is similar to the keyword description of the number, or a number. This is to put you into a "zone" or "space" of that particular number. Each number has a place or is an area or field of experience of your life and the number gets you to focus on that part of you.

The session then proceeds to take you into the qualities that need to be developed or worked on in this area of your life and also the tendencies that you need to leave behind. These qualities are the ones in alignment with your mid-heaven or the house of your horoscope your sun (your identity) is placed in according to the time of your birth.

So if the session you are working on is not about your sun sign or your mid-heaven sign you will still have it somewhere in your horoscope so it is still valuable for you to address these issues no matter whether it is prominent or not in your chart.

There is then an appropriate affirmation that you can use to facilitate the process of integrating the energy of the number and astrological associations of planets and signs.

After that comes the crystals to use in the session to also assist you with integrating, or assimilating the qualities of the session. Since we are ALL of the signs to greater or lesser degrees it is helpful and beneficial to integrate all the numbers and their associations into yourself to create inner harmony and empowerment.

This is then followed by a strategy that is similar to the quality of the number and its astrological association of sign and planet. After this is the physical symptom that indicates that these energies are not being expressed positively or normally. A physical imbalance is how the body tells us that we are doing something wrong, or at least something that causes it to malfunction. Then to assist you to positively express these energies in your life some Australian

Bush Flower Essences and meditation techniques are suggested.

It is then suggested that when you finish your meditation that you journal your experiences you had in the meditation after each session. When you have completed all nine sessions then go back over your journal entries and uncover the things you have even kept secret from yourself. You will find that these entries will give you a whole picture of what you are doing, why you are doing it, and how you can change for the better.

These nine sessions of self-discovery into the infinity of who you are will be the biggest adventure you will ever take.

It is my hope that you will see that the possibilities of everything is within you – not anything external.

We are continually led away from ourselves – distracted from our own truth and purpose. Take back your power, your life, your potentials, your dreams, and your love of life – GO WITHIN

When used with sincere intent these sessions are very powerful in bringing balance, harmony and fulfillment into your life. Ask yourself how much of your life is lived seeking externally? When you seek internally as these sessions are encouraging you to do, you expand so you become everything. The external world is merely a barometer of what is happening (or not happening) inside. If you are not having a happy experience then something needs to be learned or healed and you need to 'see' what it is and acknowledge that you created it, and heal it.

PART 2
A COURSE IN SELF EMPOWERMENT

THIS COURSE TEACHES LIFE SKILLS AND MEDITATION INCORPORATING THE ASCENSION TOOLS OF ASTROLOGY, NUMEROLOGY, FLOWER AND SPIRITUAL ESSENCES.

IF YOU HAVE THE COURAGE TO GO BEYOND WHERE YOU ARE, THESE 9 EXCITING ADVENTURES INTO POSSIBILITY ARE FOR YOU.

Well, why should we bother ourselves with self-empowerment……..?

During the course of my lifetime so far I have watched the people that don't develop their inherent talents and abilities, for whatever reason, and I have to say, based on the results they experienced, I am unable to recommend this apathetic approach to life.

The people that don't bother themselves with SELF EMPOWERMENT and ASCENSION, will find much more difficulties and frustration in their lives than those that do!

Self- empowerment and development is what life was created for. The lifetime of a person is to overcome the influence of the ego, the separating agent from the 'all that is'. The ego is what 'compares' and finds you wanting…… it perpetuates the illusion that you are separate and isolated from the whole.

In our short lives we all have the task, generally speaking, to lessen the influence of the ego and listen to our soul and spirit so that they can be expressed. I believe when this is allowed to happen, then a successful life has been lived.

So, in that light let us begin ……………

SESSION ONE

Who Am I?

"Our deepest fear is not that we are inadequate. Our deepest fear is that we are powerful beyond all measure. It is our light, not our darkness, that most frightens us.

We ask ourselves: "Who am I to be brilliant, talented and fabulous?

Actually, who are you not to be? You are a child of God. Your playing small doesn't serve the world. There is nothing enlightened about shrinking so that other people will not feel insecure around you. We were born to manifest the glory of God that is within us. It is not just in some of us; it is in everyone.

As we let our own light shine, we unconsciously give other people permission to do the same. As we are liberated from our deepest fear, our presence automatically liberates others.

This, then is our one purpose in life, to discover who we truly are and to be all that we can be."

That quotation is from Nelson Mandela's inaugural speech, written by Marianne Williamson.

So if you are just practicing 'damage control' and just 'staying out of trouble', living in perpetual fear, doubt and insecurity, then maybe you should reconsider your life strategy and come out of the corner that you are hiding in……..

"Imagine a world with ten million awakened people – fully awake – not just as a belief or an idea, but who have mastered fear, who no longer live in doubt, whatsoever, and are busy creating universes that mirror perfectly the Kingdom of Heaven. Imagine it – if you dare!" Jeshua, Way of the Heart.

So let us now look at the things that have an affinity with the Number One and the SELF.

The Number One 1......

The positive qualities of the Number One 1 are:- pioneering, leadership, activity, courage, positivity and will-power.

The negative qualities of the Number One 1 are:- selfishness, arrogance, anger, frustration, irritability and bumptiousness.

The Number One 1 has an affinity with the Planet Mars, which rules the Astrology Sign of Aries and the First House of the Zodiac and also the Masculine Principle.

To go more deeply into the Number One 1, Aries and the Planet Mars as well as the First House, you may refer to the appropriate sections of this book regarding them.

Those people who were born between the hours of 4am to 6am, or those with an Aries

North Node or the North Node in the First House, or an Aries Midheaven need to work in the area(s) of:-

*independence
*self-awareness
*courage
*constructive self-interest
*being self-determining

Tendencies to leave behind are:-

*tit-for-tat mentality
*being Mr or Mrs Nice
*being a people pleaser
*being indecisive – looking for others to decide for them
*seeing oncsclf through the eyes of others

Affirmation: "I CAN HELP OTHERS BY TRULY BEING MY BEST SELF."

KNOW WHO YOU ARE – this is essential to you, because you will have direction and purpose for why you are here, to have the feeling that you belong. Obtain your horoscope and investigate its meaning yourself, or seek counsel with an astrologer. DARE TO KNOW YOURSELF!

The crystals that assist the energy of the One or Mars/Aries, or the integration of the masculine are:

Hematite (iron ore)
Amber
Rhodachrosite

The Sign of Aries is always SOMEWHERE IN EVERYONE'S HOROSCOPE and the house it sits on the cusp of is where new growth and development is needed to be cultivated, and also the development of independence is needed in this area of their life.

The Aries Mid-heaven is when your spiritual direction is one of learning the positive qualities of the One 1 (self) or Aries in the course of your career, social status, ambitions, goals or achievements.

THE LIFE STRATEGY THAT EMPOWERS THE ARIES/MARS OR ONE 1 ENERGY IS:-

STRATEGY # ONE (1) – "GET REAL" Dr Phil McGraw.

"You have got to GET REAL to HEAL!

So, to put that realisation into motion LIFE REWARDS ACTION – awareness without subsequent action is worthless. You have to DO something about it, you have to take action of some kind.

'We do not deal much in facts when we are contemplating ourselves' Mark Twain."

..Quotes from the book "Life Strategies" by Dr Phillip C. McGraw.

Ask yourself the hard questions and give yourself the hard answers. CONFRONT YOUR PROBLEMS NOT OTHER PEOPLE.

The Aries/Mars Number One 1 physical problems when the energy isn't expressed positively are:-

The classic one is the headache, which is self invalidation. Migraines are resentment about being driven and not communicating that you don't like being told what to do.

Others are problems with the face or brains, fevers or inflammatory diseases, accidents (no patience and hostility towards the self).

So if any of the above are happening to you, you can do something to bring yourself back into balance by taking......

THE AUSTRALIAN BUSH FLOWER ESSENCES!!!

The flower essences that balance these problems are:-

*MOUNTAIN DEVIL
*BLACK-EYED SUSAN
*DOG ROSE OF THE WILD FORCES
*RED HELMET ORCHID
*ISOPOGON
*RED GREVILLEA
*EMERGENCY ESSENCE

(I must point out that the flower essences are not a substitute for medical treatment.)

Now here's the thing, the flower essences DO NOT DO IT FOR YOU AS NOTHING DOES. The flower essences heal and hold you in balance so you are more in a position to BE YOUR TRUE SELF – BUT IT IS YOU WHO MUST MAKE THAT CHOICE.

YOU ARE ACCOUNTABLE FOR YOUR LIFE AND EVERYTHING IN IT!!!

YOU DO CREATE YOUR REALITY

To become empowered you are going to have to stop BLAMING others and JUSTIFYING negative results in your life.

THAT IS EMPOWERMENT!

The spiritual journey simply consists of ceasing to be an enemy of ourselves and recognising that you are the God-Force within. Affirm that several times a day. Say "I AM THE GOD-FORCE WITHIN".

Maybe you can't necessarily feel it at first, so just imagine it in the meantime.

That is one of the first steps in reclaiming your power. If you don't like what you have in your life, then change yourself and your life will also change for the better.

Ask yourself where are your desires and wants and needs coming from, then answer with honour and truthfulness – do you really need them?

"When you are helping yourself first, that is when you are helping your world." Annette Noontil.

You are now invited to take the Australian Bush Flower Essence Meditation Mix and go into meditation examining your life and the changes you want to make to it..........

Just sit quietly. You might like to say a protection prayer of your choice (you can make it up yourself) and then take some nice deep relaxing breaths. Five to ten minutes is fine to start with, you can increase it or not as you feel comfortable.

It is important that you don't worry yourself with the small details of how what you want for you life can be gained, just what you want for your life. Or, maybe its what you want to leave your life so it can be improved.

When you are finished your meditation (your connection to your real self), then write or "journal" what came to you.

So many people are rushing past their lives, doing things that don't support who they really are. Are you doing that?

"MAY THE FORCE BE WITH YOU......"

SESSION TWO

THIS SESSION IS DEDICATED TO PACHAMAMA, THE LIVING SPIRIT OF EARTH AND THE MOTHER OF US ALL………

The Number Two (2) has an affinity with the Moon, which rules the Astrology Sign of Cancer (nurturing) and the Fourth House of the horoscope (home and family) and the Feminine Principle.

The positive qualities of the Number Two (2) are:-

*receptivity
*sensitivity
*diplomacy
*gentleness
*rhythm

The negative qualities are:-

*apathy

*slyness
*pessimism
*shyness
*sulkiness

It is my suggestion and recommendation that you read the book "INITIATION" by Elizabeth B. Jenkins, published by G.P. Putnam's Sons.

Those people who were born between the hours of 10pm to midnight, or with a Cancer North Node, or the North Node in the Fourth house, or a Cancer Midheaven, need to work in the areas of :-

*Self-nurturance and supporting others
*Staying centered in ones own feelings
*Building your own emotional foundation and security
*Honest disclosure of feelings and insecurities, particularly within intimate relationships

Tendencies to leave behind:-

*Feeling responsible for everything
*Hiding feelings and fears, keeping them a secret and manipulating the situation instead of honest disclosure.
*Needing to control everything and everyone (that's very insecure!)

AFFIRMATION: "Its okay to let my feelings show"

"most of us love from our need to love….. most of us comfort because we need comforting." NIKKI GIOVANNI

The feminine (magnetic) nature of the Two and the Moon energy also relates to our past fears and phobias and the subconscious, so there is a lot for you to uncover here. The Moon is our emotional responses based on past experiences.

I challenge you to get to know these areas

of your life! Most particularly the men because without acknowledgement of your feelings and allowing your sensitive side expression you can't empower yourself. Yes, you have a FEMININE SIDE as well as a MASCULINE SIDE regardless of your gender!!

The crystals that assist the integration of the feminine side of our nature are:-

Moonstone
Pearl
Smokey Quartz
Black Obsidian

The sign of Cancer is always somewhere in everyone's horoscope and the house it sits on the cusp of is where you need growth through instruction and training to overcome the deep subconscious emotions that have been suppressed. This house tells you where you need to use the positive qualities of your Sun Sign to do this.

The sign of Cancer is a very difficult sign to transmute and heal because of its emotional nature, and habits that have been engaged in. These dysfunctional habits must be replaced with functional habits.

The Cancer Midheaven is when your spiritual direction is one of learning the positive qualities of the Two (2) and the Sign of Cancer (emotional security and nurturing issues) in the course of your career (or the lack of), social status, ambitions, goals and achievements.

THE LIFE STRATEGY OF THE #TWO IS-

"YOU EITHER GET IT, OR YOU DON'T" Dr Phil McGraw.

Because the Two/Moon/Cancer/Feminine energy is so emotionally and subconsciously ruled, being overwhelmed by the emotions doesn't give you objectivity, and, well you become a bit thick on account that when

nothing else works ......then crying and being a victim/martyr gives you a perceived relief........the perpetual cry baby always in denial of the part you yourself is playing in creating your own problems.!!!!!

Or, it can go the other way where the feeling nature and the sensitive side is denied.

Become one of those who get it. If you aren't one of the ones who get it, then you are not coming from a position of knowledge and strength.

When you belong to an "informed minority" because you have bothered to go and find out how to' get it', you will see that the rest of the herd continue to plod on in a blind trial and error fashion!

The Sign of Cancer/Moon/# Two physical problems when the energy is not expressed positively are:-

The classic one is the stomach, when you aren't FEELING right or are anxious (fear) the stomach turns acid. The stomach holds nourishment and digests ideas, there maybe a problem with assimilating the new in your life. Other problems are, breasts (surpressing emotions, "get it off your chest"), digestion, uterus, and sickness in infancy.

So if any of the above are happening to you, you can do something to bring yourself back into balance with the Australian Bush Flower Essences.

However, I must of course point out to you that these essences are in no way a substitute for medical treatment, they are simply something additional you can do for yourself if you want to 'GET IT'.

The Flower Essences to balance these problems are:-

SHE OAK
CROWEA
PAW PAW
GREY SPIDER FLOWER
FLANNEL FLOWER
BOTTLEBRUSH
DOG ROSE OF THE WILD FORCES
RED SUVA FRANGIPANI
STURT DESERT PEA

You are now invited to take the WHITE LIGHT SPIRITUAL ESSENCE OF WATER and go into meditation to examine your feeling life to see if anything needs healing and attending to.

Before meditation always say a protection prayer of your choice and take the phone off the hook.

May your guides, angels and higher self protect you on this journey…………

SESSION THREE

This poem is from "Love Makes The Worlds Go Around. The Living Planets Speak - A book of Planetary Inspiration." By Martin Lass.

"You are a star child, borne of Love, borne of light, fashioned from star stuff.

You have a galaxy inside you, filled with living planets, fiery comets and spinning stars, filled with an eternal dance of colour, music and rhythm, filled with the love, light and hope of your Creator.

You are a Creator in embryo, an infant star traveller, on a journey towards oneness.

Your destiny is to shine.

The Solar System."

The Number Three 3 has an affinity with the Planet Mercury, which rules the Third

House of the Zodiac and the Astrological Sign of Gemini.

The positive qualities of the Number Three 3 are:-

*joy
*creativity
*inspiration and imagination
*networking
*social-ability

The negative qualities are:-
*wastefulness
*hypocrisy
*superficiality
*triviality
*worrying

Those people who were born between midnight and 2 am, or with a Gemini North Node or North Node in the Third House, or a Gemini Midheaven need to work in the areas of –

*Education and/or learning to communicate
*Listening (not just to others, but also to your life)
*Developing a healthy curiosity
*Openness to new ideas and experiences
*Seeing both sides of a situation

Tendencies to leave behind are:-

*Self-righteousness
*Lack of commitment
*Taking shortcuts
*Careless spontaneity
*Closed belief systems that don't allow new information to enter them.

AFFIRMATION: "If I don't understand, its okay to ask questions."

The Three energy is very much mental (Air) energy and it facilitates the freedom of expression and creativity of the mind.

The energy of the planet Mercury is how we think, what our attitudes are and how we communicate. Now ask yourself is all of that in fear, or is it in love.

I challenge you to examine your thinking, is it in good health and balance, does it have clarity and focus, or is it otherwise?

The crystals that assist the integration of this mental air energy are:-

Agate
Adventurine
Citrine
Fluorite

The Sign of Gemini is always somewhere in everyone's horoscope, and the house it sits on the cusp of is where you need to develop curiosity, or become more inquisitive. This curiosity will help you grow and educate yourself in this particular area of your life.

The Gemini Midheaven is when your spiritual direction is towards the positive qualities of the sign, the Number Three 3 (communication and educational issues) in the course of your career (or the lack of), social status, ambitions, goals and achievements.

THE LIFE STRATEGY OF THE # THREE IS:-

"THERE IS NO REALITY: ONLY YOUR PERCEPTION." Dr Phil McGraw.

"There is nothing either good or bad, but thinking makes it so." William Shakespear.

So, identify the filters through which you view the world. Ask yourself how is your perception influenced by your belief systems. Where did those belief systems come from and do they serve you well, or not?

You have a choice as to how you perceive an experience, is it –

Good	Bad
Negative	Positive
Acceptance	Non Acceptance
Fortunate	Unfortunate
Empowering	Dis-empowering

How is your perception affecting you??

If you look back on your life you may find in retrospect, that at the time they happened, some of the things you deemed 'bad' weren't. Later on you may see that if that 'bad' thing hadn't happened to you, something much worse would have.

Some things are blessings in disguise.

The sign of Gemini, the Planet Mercury and the #3 physical problems, when the energy is not expressed positively are:-

Energy blocks in the shoulders, arms, hands,

lungs, bronchial tubes, thymus gland, lack of oxygenation of the body through hampered breathing, nerves and intestinal trouble.

So if any of the above are happening to you, you can do something to bring yourself back into balance with the Australian Bush Flower Essences. (These in no way take the place of medical treatment however).

I will also point out that no flower essence has any side affects whatsoever, so you have nothing to lose.

The Flower Essences are:-

ISOPOGON
JACARANDA
BUSH FUCHSIA
BORONIA
FRESHWATER MANGROVE
ANGELSWORD
SUNDEW
STURT DESERT PEA

SUNSHINE WATTLE

You are now invited to take the WHITE LIGHT SPIRITUAL ESSENCE of AIR and go into meditation to examine the way you think – does it serve you well? Is it from fear and doubt, or it is from love and trust?

SESSION FOUR

"In the infinity of life where I am,
All is perfect, whole and complete.
I accept perfect health as the natural state
of my being.
I now consciously release any mental
patterns within me that could express as
dis-ease in any way.
I love and approve of myself.
I love and approve of my body.
I feed it nourishing foods and beverages.
I exercise it in ways that are fun.
I recognize my body as a wonderous and
magnificent machine,
and I feel privileged to live in it.
I love lots of energy.
All is well in my world."

The above quote is from "You Can Heal Your Life." By Louise Hay.

1. If you don't already have this book I have just quoted from then it is my strong

recommendation that you obtain it as soon as possible. Your body tells you what you need to learn.

2. When you have obtained this book look up any physical problems you may have and then address the appropriate mental pattern or emotional causation that is at the root of that problem.

The physical body is our vehicle for spiritual growth and physical problems are the barometer of the soul.

When you fall in love with your glorious imperfections that's when you really start to live.

So let us now look at the things that have an affinity with the # Four 4.

The # Four 4 has an affinity with the Planet Venus, which rules the sign of Taurus and the Second House of the Zodiac.

The positive qualities of the # Four 4 are:-

•practicality
•endurance
•being organised
•economy
•worthiness

The negative qualities of the # Four 4 are:-

•plodding
•narrowness
•possessiveness
•rigidity
•jealousy

Those people who were born between the hours of 2am to 4am, or those with a Taurus North Node or North Node in the Second House, or a Taurus midheaven need to work in the areas of:-

•Developing a sense of self-worth and inner security

•Developing gratitude
•Cultivating an awareness of personal values
•Developing an awareness of nurturing from Mother Earth
•Developing detachment

The tendencies to leave behind are:-

•Being resistant to change
•Over concern with other peoples business
•Obsessive or compulsive tendencies
•Resentment
•Being indulgent

AFFIRMATION: "When I satisfy my own needs and the expressed needs of others, I build a stable base for relationships."

Success is achieved when the practical side of the nature is developed and laziness is overcome. Procrastination is also something that is prominent with the 4/Taurus/Venus energy.

Also, developing a good connection to Mother Earth and then a good connection to Father Sky, being a bridge between the two, in harmony with both is empowering. When this happens the Crown Chakra is open to receive energies and inspirations from the Cosmos, as well as the Root Chakra being open to connect to the Earth.

Connection causes balance.

The crystals that assist the energy of the Four/Venus/Taurus and the integration of the Earth energy are:-

Carnelian
Jade
Brown Jasper
Emerald

The Sign of Taurus is always somewhere in everyone's horoscope, and the house it sits on the cusp of is where you need to be productive and to see the actual results of your productivity.

The Taurus Midheaven is when your spiritual direction is one of learning the positive qualities of the Sign, (detachment and self-worth) and the # Four in the course of your career, social status, ambitions, goals or achievements.

LIFE STATEGY # FOUR 4

"YOU HAVE TO NAME IT TO CLAIM IT!" Dr Phil McGraw.

Life gives you what you have the courage to ask for or demand for yourself. Get clear about what you want so you can place your order.

It isn't okay to not know what you want out of life and your horoscope does give clues for this through the Venus and Mars placements.

If you don't know what you want you can't

be contributing to your own life and the lives of others, and you can't be coming from love and trust. All you have to do is to have the intention of wanting to know what you want, and then NAME IT and be specific.

The Universe does deliver but it must know (from you) what it is.

So I guess you have to ask….. Do you want to waste your life just mucking around, or do you want to NAME IT TO CLAIM IT and live your life with purpose and meaning?

Just a watch-point about NAMING IT TO CLAIM IT.

Quite often we think we know what we want, but really we don't. We may want a new car, a house, to be married, to have children, to go on a holiday, etc. etc. etc…….

But what we really want is the FEELING

we think these things will give to us. When we get whatever it was that we wanted we sometimes find that is wasn't what we wanted after all for this reason.

Ask yourself……
1.   What do you want?
2.   What must you do to have it?
3.   How would you feel when you had it?

So, what you really want is what you described in question 3.

If you need to go deeper then repeat 1.2. and 3. again.

The Taurus/Venus/# Four 4 physical problems when the energy isn't expressed positively are:-

Problems in the neck, throat, thyroid gland, kidneys, pancreas.

So if you are experiencing any of the above you can do something to bring yourself back into balance by taking the following Australian Bush Flower Essences. These essences are in no way a replacement for medical treatment.

OLD MAN BANKSIA
BAUHINIA
FIVE CORNERS
BORONIA
BUSH FUCHSIA
PINK MULLA MULLA
SILVER PRINCESS
PEACH FLOWER TEA TREE

You are now invited to take the White Light Essence EARTH and go into meditation to examine what YOU WANT for your life and also to seek insight into any physical problems you may have.

May The Force be with you……..

A MESSAGE FROM THE GUIDANCE REALM.

PEACE WITHIN YOURSELF WILL BRING PEACE TO OTHERS.

LOVE WITHIN YOURSELF WILL BRING LOVE TO OTHERS.

GRATITUDE WITHIN YOURSELF WILL BRING GRATITUDE TO OTHERS.

THESE THINGS I TELL YOU, AND THE LACK THEREOF, IS THE REASON FOR THE TROUBLES YOU NOW HAVE IN YOUR WORLD.

THE LACK OF PEACE, LOVE AND GRATITUDE WITHIN YOURSELVES DISRUPTS THE ENERGY IN THE GUIDANCE REALM ALSO. THE FORCES OF DARKNESS NEED TO BE INTEGRATED AND OWNED BY EACH PERSON, FOR WE CREATE THEM AS MUCH AS WE CREATE THE GOODNESS IN OUR LIVES.

WHEN THERE IS BALANCE THERE IS HARMONY.

I LEAVE YOU TO CONTEMPLATE THIS………

ANOTHER MESSAGE FROM THE GUIDANCE REALM…..

THIS THING YOU CALL GOD IS NOT A BEING AND SHOULD NEVER BE WORSHIPPED AS BEING ONE.

FOR THE FORCE THAT PEOPLE CALL GOD IS NOTHING BUT PURE ENERGY THAT PEOPLE AND GOVERNMENTS HAVE USED FOR THEIR OWN ENDS.

THE TRUE MEANING HAS BEEN LOST FOR GOD IS EVERYTHING AND IT IS NOTHING.

SESSION FIVE

"When we are in contact with our hearts, our egos rest upon a foundation which does not secure ourselves at the expense of other people, but which instead promotes our loving capacities. When we are illuminated by our inner light, we radiate a warmth which includes and embraces the people around us and enables them as well as us to shine."
Tracey Marks.

The Number Five has an affinity with the Astrology Sign of Leo, which is ruled by the Sun and the Fifth House of the Zodiac.

The positive qualities of the #5 are:-

• The love of freedom
• Vitality for life
• Resourcefulness
• Progression
• Promotion

The negative qualitites of the #5 are:-

•Perversion
•Bad Taste
•Sensationalism
•Restlessness/carelessness
•Being a rolling stone

Those people who were born between the hours of 8pm to 10pm, or those with a Leo North Node or the North Node in the Fifth House or a Leo Midheaven need to work in the areas of:-

•Following one's hearts desires
•Self-confidence and creative self-expression
•Enjoying life- having fun
•A willingness to takc ccntre-stage or leadership roles
•Opening the heart centre

Tendencies to leave behind are:-

•Aloofness

•Yielding to peer pressure in order to 'belong'
•Emotional detachment and isolation
•Cold or hard heartedness
•Endless superficial/meaningless socialising

AFFIRMATION: "The only person who can create my happiness is me."

"In Galactic Astrology the Sun represents a centre of consciousness, usually self-consciousness and ego-consciousness. It is the place we identify with as "I" or "me". The stars and constellations represent the dimensions of the soul and spirit. The stars are out all the time, yet we cannot see them during the day because the Sun is too bright. The stars appear when the Sun goes down. MULTIDIMENSIONAL REALITIES APPEAR WHEN THE EGO IS TRANSCENDED. During solar eclipses, the Sun (and ego) are temporarily blocked out. The stars can actually be seen during the day at the moment of a total solar eclipse.

The archetypal Lion is the 'ruler of the heart" for each individual. Often this archetype is projected onto a celebrity, such as a member of a royal family, a rock star, or a movie star. Integrating this for yourself involves being open to the Lion and being willing to experience your heart as the ruler; in other words, always doing what you truly want and acting out of love rather than fear." From the article "Keys under the Sphinx" by Ray Mardyks.

The crystals that assist the energy of the Five/Leo/Sun energy are:-

Rose quartz
Chrysoprase
Kunzite
Ruby

The sign Leo is always somewhere in everyone's horoscope and the house cusp it sits on is where you feel a need for personal development and self expression. If you use the positive qualities of your sun sign in the affairs of this house, you will feel a deep sense of inner peace and contentment.

The Leo midheaven (10th House cusp) is when your spiritual direction is one of learning the positive qualities of your sun sign, the #5 and Leo (confidence, creativity and leadership), in the course of your career, social status, ambitions, goals or achievements.

LIFE STRATEGY # FIVE (5)

"YOU CAN'T CHANGE WHAT YOU DON'T ACKNOWLEDGE" Dr Phil McGraw.

I have met very few people who have self love (not ego, I've met plenty of those!).

People who go around with the "everything is wonderful and lovely" are usually in denial and aren't being honest.

Be honest with yourself about what isn't working in your life and stop making excuses and justifying it. In fact self-honour is what opens the heart chakra – to honour the self, and when you do that you automatically honour all life.

If you won't take ownership of your role in a situation, then you cannot and will not change it.

So own up and stop denying and defending and HONOUR YOURSELF WITH THE TRUTH about the part you are playing, and give yourself real answers so you can start to manage the problem or situation into balance.

The Number Five/Lco/Sun physical problems when this energy isn't expressed positively are:-

Low vitality/poor recuperative powers
Heart problems
Body heat/perspiration

Back
Spine

So if any of the above are happening to you, you can do something to bring yourself back into balance by taking The Australian Bush Flower Essences. However, these flower essences in no way take the place of medical treatment.

The flower essences that balance these problems are:-

BLUEBELL
HIBBERTIA
TALL MULLA MULLA
STURT DESERT ROSE
ILLAWARRA FLAME TREE
BANKSIA ROBUR
LITTLE FLANNEL FLOWER
TURKEY BUSH
CHRISTMAS BELL

When you are projecting a loving heart,

creativity and self expression flow out and you automatically focus on what you can give, instead of what you can take, thereby contributing everywhere you go. When people have open hearts, unconditional love creates your natural abundance.

You are now invited to take the White Light Essence FIRE and to go into meditation asking your spirit to give you guidance. Go into your heart and see how you can bring more joy and abundance into your life and allow your heart centre to let the universal love flow freely through it ………..

You may ask the question "Is what I do in my life honouring myself" if you wish, its optional.

Remember before meditation always say a protection prayer of your choice and take the phone off the hook.

May peace be unto you……………

SESSION SIX

DO I HAVE ENOUGH INNER PEACE TO SERVE OTHERS??

The Number SIX 6……..

The positive qualities of the Number Six 6 are:-

- Balance,
- adjustment,
- love,
- domestic harmony,
- sympathy/understanding,
- service to others.

The negative qualities are:-

- "Slavery",
- anxiety/worry,
- meddlesomeness,
- drudgery,
- conventionality,
- servitude.

The desire for harmony and everything to be smooth and orderly often lends itself to the pursuit of singing or playing a musical instrument.

Kindness, tolerance and co-operation are the lessons for this number.

The Number Six 6 has an affinity with the planets Venus and Mercury, which rule the astrology signs of Libra and Virgo and the Seventh and Sixth houses of the zodiac respectively.

Those people who were born between the hours of 4pm to 8pm, or who are the signs of Libra or Virgo, or have Libra or Virgo North Nodes or the North Node in either the sixth or seventh houses of the zodiac need to develop in the areas of:-

•co-operation with others
•tolerance/acceptance of self
•being decisive

- service to others
- diplomacy and tact
- bringing order to chaos.

Tendencies to leave behind are:-

- vagueness/inaction
- feelings of inadequacy
- selfishness
- over-concern with survival
- self-centredness

Affirmation: "WHEN I FOCUS AND HAVE A PLAN, THE WHOLE UNIVERSE OPENS THE PATHWAY TO SUCCESS."

And/or

"WHEN I SHARE WITH OTHERS I HAVE MORE".

The mental energy of the #6 is very oriented towards relationships, family and community and the planet Mercury (rules Virgo). The planet Venus (rules Libra) is more the harmony and balance side of the desire for fairness and justice, and harmonious relating.

The crystals that assist the energy of the Six or Virgo/Libra energy and the process of self-healing are:-

MOSS AGATE
HOWLITE
RHODACHROSITE
ADVENTURINE

The signs of Libra and Virgo are always somewhere in everyone's horoscope and the house they sit on the cusp of is where you

a) Libra – need to regain balance in the affairs of this house.
b) Virgo – need to " discard the chaff from the wheat". There is a need to analyse your feelings in regard to the affairs of this house and develop a more practical and systematic approach to achieve

harmony.

The Libra and Virgo Midheaven is when your spiritual direction is one of learning the positive qualities of the Six 6 (healing/acceptance) in the course of your career, social status, ambitions, goals or achievements.

THE LIFE STRATEGY THAT EMPOWERS THE SIX LIBRA/VIRGO ENERGY IS:-

"WE TEACH PEOPLE HOW TO TREAT US." Dr Phil McGraw.

Once again we must own our part in what makes others treat us the way they do. If you have an abusive relationship with someone where they treat you badly, it is up to YOU to re-negotiate with them, or set boundaries that prevent them from abusing you. If you allow them to treat you badly they will. So, stop allowing them to behave that way towards you. You must also look at WHY you allowed them to abuse you and be honest with yourself.

Stop blaming them and respond to their treatment of you so it stops being abusive and starts being respectful, kind and honourable.

By doing this you are creating a win/win situation and can heal yourself as well as others.

YOUMUSTHEALWHYYOUPERCEIVE YOU SHOULD BE TREATED BADLY.

The Number Six 6 Libra/Virgo, Mercury/ Venus physical problems when the energy isn't expressed in a balanced positive way are:-

Problems with intestines
food assimilation
duodenum
kidneys
filtration of body fluids or urine.

So if any of these things are malfunctioning in your life then you can do something to bring yourself back into balance by taking the AUSTRALIAN BUSH FLOWER ESSENCES…….However I must point out that the flower essences are not substitutes for medical treatment.

The flower essences that balance these problems are:-

BOTTLEBRUSH
KAPOK BUSH
CROWEA
DOG ROSE
PEACH FLOWER TEA TREE
PAW PAW
YELLOW COWSLIP ORCHID
PHILOTHECA

You must treat yourself well FIRST, then others will also treat you well.

I invite you now to shift the way you relate

to your life and look at how effectively, or not, you are living it. Are you just spinning your wheels? Are you "wounded" and going around "contaminating" your life, or is your life contributing in some way?

You are now invited to take the Australian Bush Flower Essence Combination mix of EMERGENCY ESSENCE and go into meditation to heal your fears, worries and anxieties in your life and any relationships where you aren't being treated harmoniously.

Always say a protection prayer of your choice before meditating.

When you finish your meditation it will help if you write in your journal what came up for you in your meditation. When you have completed all the nine sessions you will be able to see from your journal entries just what things need to be worked on in your life.

May you find insights into your own self healing and inner peace be yours…………

SESSION SEVEN

What must I change to empower myself?
– that is the question!

This may or may not be something tangible, it may be a belief or a perception, but it is always something about yourself and no one else.

"Courage means the power to let go of the familiar and the secure." Rollo May

The number seven has an affinity with the astrology sign of Scorpio and the planet Pluto, which rules the Eighth House of the zodiac.

All these have one thing in common, they are all the energy of transformation, change and rebirth.

The positive qualities of the # 7 are:-

•trust

- refinement
- spirituality
- introspection
- poise
- technicality.

The negative qualities of the #7 are:-

•sarcasm
•melancholy
•skepticism
•suppression
•faithlessness

The biggest challenge for the number seven people is to use their power for the highest good of all and not negatively to control.

Those people who were born between the hours of 2pm to 4pm, or those with a Scorpio North Node or the North Node in the 8th House or a Scorpio Midheaven need to work in the areas of ....

•Enjoying things without having to own them

•Having the conscious intention to develop self empowerment

•Proactively embracing change as the only constant in life

•Letting go of past situations, resentments and grievances, to learn forgiveness to break the bonds of the past

The tendencies to leave behind are:-

•Having the same routine for years and stubbornly holding on to it

•Being possessive

•Seeking power from external sources (addiction)

AFFIRMATION: "The alternative to change is stagnation".

Authentic power comes from within and so does security, so accumulating material things or possessiveness of others will only cause further insecurity, and none of these things can be taken with you when you pass over. The only things you take with you when you pass over are your spiritual growth and evolution.

The crystals that assist the integration of change and transformation of the #7 Scorpio are:-

Alexandrite
Lepidolite
Black Opal
Topaz

The sign of Scorpio is always somewhere in everyone's horoscope, and the house it sits on the cusp of is where you will have an intense desire to delve deeply into the affairs of this house.

THE LIFE STRATEGY that empowers the # 7, Scorpio, Pluto, 8th House energy is:-

"THERE IS POWER IN FORGIVENESS"

Dr Phil McGraw.

The power in forgiveness is that it releases you from the bondage of resentments, hate, negative feelings and emotions which block what power you can create for yourself. Power comes from love (creative energy), whereas the opposite, hate is destructive energy. Now I don't know about you, but I would want to distance myself from destruction and instead invite love and creativity into my life.

You forgive for yourself, not the other person, so you can move on and not be held back or blocked by negative emotions.

It may help to look at what was the gift that the negative experience showed you, or what was it that you learned from it, and take that gift with you and move on using that gift to empower yourself in the future.

It is recommended that you read "The Seat

of The Soul" by Gary Zukav for further investigation into forgiveness and the subject of authentic power.

When the 7/Scorpio/Pluto 8th House energy isn't expressed positively then the nose, bladder, sex organs, adenoids, bowels malfunction. So if any of these things are happening to you, you can bring yourself back into balance by taking THE AUSTRALIAN BUSH FLOWER ESSENCES.

These essences are in no way a substitute for medical treatment.

They are:-

DAGGAR HAKEA
STURT DESERT ROSE
BILLY GOAT PLUM
BUSH IRIS
SOUTHERN CROSS
MINT BUSH

BAUHINIA

These essences facilitate transformation and regeneration by balancing the consciousness naturally, making the change easier for the person to see life in a loving and enlightened way, thus healing the trauma, so it can be LET GO OF. The person can move on, creating their life in love, peace and joy.

The Pluto energy causes upheaval so inner wisdom can be gained and evolutionary growth is then possible.

You are now invited to take the WHITE LIGHT ANGELIC ESSENCE to facilitate any forgiveness that is needed in your life – particularly if it is yourself you need to forgive.

Just relax and breath deeply to allow yourself the space to feel safe to examine who or what you need to release yourself from to move forward.........

May The Force, your guides and your Higher Self assist you with this process.

SESSION EIGHT

"My feelings can't quite venture out, I'm filled with memories and doubt, I think I'd rather do without, than take a chance."
Cryer and Ford.

AM I ABLE TO RESPOND TO MY LIFE WHEN REQUIRED?

OR

DO I FAIL TO?

Let us now look at the things that have an affinity with the Number Eight 8 and being responsive to life.

The positive qualities of the Number Eight are:-

• Organisation
• Authority (over the self)
• The power to succeed
• Self-reliance

•Management abilities

The negative qualities of the Number Eight are:-

•Demand for recognition
•Ambition for self or greed
•Scheming
•Revenge
•Oppressiveness

The # 8 has an affinity with the Planet Saturn, which rules the Astrology sign of Capricorn and the Tenth House of the Zodiac.

To go more deeply into Capricorn, the Planet Saturn as well as the Tenth House you may refer to the appropriate sections of this book.

Those people who were born between 10am and 12 noon, or those with a Capricorn North Node, or the North Node in the Tenth House, or a Capricorn Mid Heaven need to work in the areas of:-

• Maturity
• Self-Respect
• Becoming and staying goal oriented
• Taking personal responsibility for your own life
• Developing emotional security

Tendencies to leave behind are:-

• Controlling others through being emotionally fearful
• Living too much in the past and too much at home (afraid to leave home)
• Moodiness
• Emotional denial and invalidation
• Emotional dependency and childishness

AFFIRMATION: "I DON'T NEED TO DEPEND ON ANYONE ELSE TO TAKE CARE OF ME."

Life is not cured its managed, so be your

own life manager and take responsibility for whatever the results of the life are.

You are the only one who has control of you, so you are the only one who is in a position to manage your life.

If for some reason you are not managing your life.......then reclaim your life from whatever or whoever does.

YOUR LIFE IS YOUR BIRTHRIGHT.

The crystals that assist the energy of the # 8, Capricorn or the Planet Saturn, or the integration of personal power in your life are:-

Ruby
Black Tourmaline
Dumortierite

The sign of Capricorn is ALWAYS SOMEWHERE IN EVERYONE'S horoscope and the house it sits on the cusp of is where we need respect and recognition, but don't actively pursue this as it can only be earned through merit (it must be commanded not demanded). There may be frustration in the affairs of this house for that reason.

The Capricorn Mid Heaven (10th House ruler) is when your spiritual direction is one of learning the positive qualities of the # 8 (life management and emotional stability, allowing the ability to respond to your life's needs), in the course of your career (or the lack of), social status, ambitions, goals or achievements.

THE LIFE STRATEGY THAT EMPOWERS THE # 8, OR CAPRICORN, SATURN ENERGY IS:-

YOU CREATE YOUR OWN REALITY 100%!

This is the most important strategy of all – if you are not willing to embrace this concept then you are choosing to be a victim.

This strategy when accepted allows you to take your power back and become able to understand that you gave your power away through ignorance, and now you are reclaiming it through intention and awareness. When you are only dealing with yourself, which is what the strategy is about, then you can reclaim your own power.

If you perceive this power was 'taken' from you then you are a victim- NO ONE IS A VICTIM.

YOU CREATE YOUR OWN REALITY

The # 8/ Saturn/ Capricorn/ 10th House physical problems when this energy isn't expressed positively in the physical body (causing a block) are:-

The classic one is inflammation of the joints or any joint problems, particularly the knees (remember the symbol for Capricorn is a goat climbing a mountain, as you need to bend your knees to do so). This is symbolic of flexibility and not rigidity!! Others are skin problems, chilling and cold, Gall Bladder, arthritis and rheumatism.

So if any of the above are happening to you, you can do something to bring your consciousness and your body back into balance by taking ......

THE AUSTRALIAN BUSH FLOWER ESSENCES

These flowers are in no way a substitute for medical treatment.

The flower essences that balance the above problems are:-

•HIBBERTIA
•ISOPOGON
•LITTLE FLANNEL FLOWER

- •ILLAWARRA FLAME TREE
- •DETOX ESSENCE (COMBINATION MIX available at Health Food Stores)
- •PINK MULLA MULLA

These physical problems indicate ("Your Body is the Barometer of Your Soul" by Annette Noontil) a consciousness that isn't flexible (joints) and feeling unloved, or a desire to blame (victim consciousness), or feelings of rejection. So, self- love and approval need to be incorporated into the life if one is experiencing these problems.

If there is a pre-occupation with 'punishment' it must be understood that there is no such thing as 'punishment' only cause and effect.

It is now suggested that you investigate learning about how you are creating your own reality, and what you need to take responsibility for in your life, so you can be more ABLE TO RESPOND TO YOUR LIFE PATH AND YOUR LIFE LESSONS in a more empowered way.

Remember whatever you have created in your life that is unwanted, can also be un-created and replaced with what you want by you, no matter what it is.

Use this session as a way of BECOMING AWARE OF YOUR LIFE and look at whether you are being a victim and giving your power away.......

You are now invited to take the WHITE LIGHT SPIRITUAL ESSENCE – DEVIC ESSENCE, and meditate in an outdoor place of natural beauty of your choice, about the nature of your own life and how it is connected to the Planet and the natural world.

Taking responsibility for your own life also helps you to care for the Earth.

May you walk in beauty and strength.

SESSION NINE

NATIVE AMERICAN PRAYER FOR PEACE

"Oh Great Spirit of our Ancestors, I raise my pipe to you.

To your messengers the four winds, and to Mother Earth who provides for your children.

Give us the wisdom to teach our children to love, to respect, and to be kind to each other so that they may grow with peace in mind.

Let us learn to share all good things that you provide for us on this Earth."

This session is about universality and the brotherhood of man, regardless of where you originate from.

WE ARE ALL ONE!!

The positive qualities of the # Nine 9 are:-

- understanding
- humanitarianism
- philanthropy
- compassion
- charity
- universal love
- the higher law

The negative qualities of the # Nine 9 are:-

- egocentricity
- immorality
- bitterness
- fickleness
- aimless dreaming

The Number Nine has an affinity with the Planet Uranus, which rules the Astrology Sign of Aquarius and the llth House of the Zodiac.

To go more deeply into the # Nine, Aquarius, the planet Uranus and the llth House, you may refer to the appropriate sections of this book.

Those people who were born between the hours of 8am to 10am, or those with an Aquarian North Node or the North Node in the llth House, or an Aquarian Mid Heaven need to work in the areas of:-

•Working towards the good of the collective
•Impersonal service to humanity
•Social reforms and cultural creativity and exchange
•Equality for all – human rights and causes
•Working to spread light and love globally
•Peace
•Individual and collective evolution

Tendencies to leave behind are:-

•Ego based desires (The ego must be transcended to express this energy)
•Poverty or victim consciousness
•Conditional behaviours
•Melodramatic tendencies
•Racial prejudice or a superiority complex

AFFIRMATION: "WHEN I DO WHAT IS BEST FOR EVERYONE INVOLVED, I WIN."

Social evolution is what the Aquarian Age is about. The first streaming to the Aquarian energy began in 1781 when Uranus was discovered. Shortly afterward the French Revolution followed and equality for all was the essence of that revolution.

Now, humankind must elevate their consciousness to achieve equality and unity for all.

The crystals that assist the energy of the Nine, Uranus, Aquarius are:-

Picture Jasper – the stone of global awareness

Lapis Lazuli – for friendship and psychic ability.

Aquamarine – for acceptance of uniqueness in self and others.

The Sign of Aquarius is always SOMEWHERE IN EVERYONE'S HOROSCOPE and the house it sits on the cusp of is where you need to obtain new knowledge in order to break down old ideas from past lifetimes. This is where the consciousness needs to be elevated.

The Aquarian Mid Heaven (10th House cusp) is when your spiritual direction is one of learning the positive qualities of the Nine (humanitarianism), in the course of your career(or the lack of), social status, ambitions, goals or achievements.

THE LIFE STRATEGY THAT EMPOWERS THE AQUARIUS/URANUS OR NINE 9 ENERGY IS:-

STRATEGY # NINE (9) – THE ONLY REASON YOU ARE ALIVE IS TO EVOLVE.

When we die the only currency we take with us from this world is evolutionary growth and spiritual development.

Hearses don't have trailers and your bank balance doesn't count for diddly squat!

So if you are one of those people who think that you were only born to pay the mortgage and that you should give up your dreams to give your children a good life, then you have got it wrong.

Do you realise you are teaching them to also do that and depriving them of their dreams.

Most of the problems of this world are caused through the disconnection of the life purpose and life lessons of the individual.

YOU CAN KNOW WHAT YOUR LIFE PURPOSE AND YOUR LIFE LESSONS ARE!

Many other problems are also caused by the disconnection to the natural world.

When the life is lived in ignorance of these things it's disast(e)rous (dis- against, aster – the stars) to the individuals who live like this and those they make contact with. The life is lived unconsciously, and without meaning, so valuable contributions are not made and the collective suffers. Very sad.

I believe we are born to heal ourselves of our own self-inflicted wounds. When we are 'wounded' we contaminate, when we are healed or made whole we are then in a position to contribute.

With the correct use of Numerology and Astrology you can become consciously aware of this vital information and use it in your life.

When you are a Nine Birthforce Number then you must first place yourself in a position of self-mastery in order to contribute to the whole through service, compassion and philanthropy.

The Nine/ Aquarius/ Uranus physical problems when the energy isn't expressed positively are:-

Nervous disorders, strange 'accidents', calves of the legs, ankles, electicity of the body, periphcral circulation, varicose veins.

So if any of thc above are happening to you, you can do something to bring yourself back into balance by taking the AUSTRALIAN BUSH FLOWER ESSENCES of:-

TALL MULLA MULLA
SYDNEY ROSE
SLENDER RICE FLOWER
TALL YELLOW TOP
PINK MULLA MULLA
STURT DESERT ROSE
FLANNEL FLOWER

These flower essences are of course not a substitute for medical treatment. However, they have no side effects, unlike medical treatments, so you have nothing to lose.

I hope these nine sessions of self-empowerment have accelerated your evolution, or at least pointed you in directions to assist you.

You are now invited to take the WHITE LIGHT SPIRITUAL ESSENCE OF HIGHER SELF, and go into meditation to connect to your higher mind, your higher knowing and your intuition.

After your meditation I also invite you to celebrate your life and its challenges by serving the Planet and those upon it in some way.

May you grow and evolve in love and peace throughout all of your days……………..

ISBN 141209459-3